These stories are loosely based on my life experiences, with modern day sass and humour (well, I think I am funny). Names have been changed to protect the guilty. This book is dedicated to the characters in my stories and to anyone who has supported me throughout all of it. Thank you all for the inspiration.

Table of Contents

Part 1
Dating in The City

To My Top Boys

Dear Don:

My first *high school boyfriend*. We were young, awkward, and shy. You told me that you "*could never break up with a girl*" and then you eventually started telling me that you could not meet up with me as your grandmother was having a birthday party, for **7 weeks in a row**, before I finally *got the hint* and ended it. This was shortly before you got suspended from school for having a **BB Gun in your locker. Thank you.**

Dear Joe:

You were the one who invited me to go **"sword shopping"** on our one and only date. You even had your sword sharpened while we were there. You then ended up locked away in a *mental health facility* later that night, for running around shirtless with **your new sword**. I always felt a little bit guilty about this, for not stopping you from sharpening your sword and all, but I hope that you got the help that you needed. I am sorry. **Thank you.**

Dear Ronny:

You took me out for *fast food burgers* on our only date. I had hope for you, with our shared interest in journalism and research, as well as the fact that you came up to me and asked for my phone number in the mall. You were ahead of me in line when we ordered our meals. You ordered for me, without asking what I wanted to eat (*I could have been a vegetarian*). You ordered yourself a burger with a side of *poutine* and a coke. You then **eyed me up and down** and said, "*you clearly don't need a drink or a side dish*", making me feel self-conscious. You asked me for cash to pay for both of our meals and then you **kept my change**. I never got over that rudeness. As an unrelated side note, you also had an annoying habit of grunting before speaking. **Thank you.**

Dear *Pigeon* Pierce:

You seemed fun. The one who could always get a dance floor started (*Pre-COVID*) and helped me get out of my shell a little bit. You shaved **10 years off of your age**, which should have been **a red flag**. It was more unfortunate, however, that **my new boss** and I walked past you, lying on the street **covered in pigeons** from head to toe, while tourists took your photograph. Thank you for not acknowledging me or shouting my name but we both know that it was not meant to be. **Thank you.**

Dear Dylan:

I had hope for you. You could make me laugh and you liked the same book author as me. You claimed to be an engineer, although I found it a little suspicious that you did not wear the pinky ring because it was "*too pretentious.*" It is very unfortunate that you **stood me up** to go to a **Taylor Swift concert by yourself.** You even dressed up like *Taylor* for the concert (*you did always say that you* *love costumes)*. I do not blame you for going to the concert, but a text message would have been nice. **Thank you.**

Dear Edwin:

I was **smitten** with you. You taught a *Bootcamp Class*; you had rock hard muscles and a soft spot for the *Backstreet Boys*. Thank you for coming to the funeral with me. I hope your film career finally took off, and you could finally leave your *grandmother's* basement. It is too bad that when we attended that dinner party for couples, you started hitting on a **married woman** in front of her husband and then **ghosted me** to focus on creating your film. **Thank you.**

Dear John:

I mean... **it was weird** when you got aggressive that I was not responding **quickly enough** to your messages, despite the fact that we had never met in person. **It was even weirder** when you arrived at our agreed meeting spot immediately, on our one *spontaneous date*, despite my warning that I was still getting dressed. You then got frustrated that you had to wait for me. **The weirdest part**, however, was during our date when you were staring silently at me, literally refusing to talk about anything or respond to any question or comment that I said, and then laughing at me whenever the **silence caused me to squirm**. You found it so amusing that I *"could not handle silence"*. I was not quite sure why I was there; you could have sat silently in a bar by yourself. I was quite sure that

you were going to **murder me** but, *thankfully,* you
did   not.   **Thank**   **you.**

Dear Andy:

Genuinely, you were the nicest guy that I ever thought that I would meet. You even helped me when I was moving apartments. You were really a *drop everything to be there for you*, type of guy. Unfortunately, you wanted to spend our **third date**, driving an hour and a half (*one way*) **with your mom along for the ride, to visit your grandmother**. You would not take *"no"* **for an answer**. The idea of making small talk with your *mom* for the **three hours round trip** was giving me anxiety, especially given that it would have been my first time meeting her. You pestered me to the point that I literally had to hideout at my parents' house just in case you showed up at my apartment, which I was quite convinced you were going to do, given the tone of the messages. It was simply **way too much for me, too fast**. I am sorry that I could not be what you needed me to be. **Thank you.**

Dear Paul:

Let's fact it, this was an uncomfortable date. After weeks of you pushing to meet up, I finally agreed. **You suggested** that we go to a **bar for dinner** and then ordered water and told the waiter that **we would not be eating**. You then stared at me while I drank my one glass of wine, as you sipped your water. It was *awkward*. You explained that this was because you **pre-drank with your friends**, though this date started at **around 5:30p.m. on a work night** (*did you pre-eat too?*). You claimed to be a *Court Reporter*, but you were unfamiliar with *legal terminology* and any current trial. You then assumed that I would go home with you and when I refused, you **blocked me. Thank you.**

Dear Sam:

The one who I thought would *"balance me out"*. You proudly weighed 550 pounds at the time that we dated, and I was struggling to move on from my strict diet. I thought that dating you would help me relax and bend the rules, although when you poured nearly an **entire jar of sugar** into your tiny cup of coffee, I started to rethink this. When seeing me once a week was not enough for you, you gave me an *ultimatum* **over text message**, that in order to keep dating you, **I had to quit the gym.** I chose the gym. **Thank you.**

Dear James:

The genius with brain damage. You looked a lot older than you claimed to be and, although you brought me flowers, you seemed **a little creepy**. You claimed that you were once a *genius* and then had a tragic car accident, **resulting in brain damage**, and now you are probably *"just slightly more intelligent"* than me. In fairness, I am not the one who shoveled the snow off the neighbours' driveways for a living and your spelling was atrocious. **Thank you.**

Dear Brian:

Another from my brain damage phase. You studied at school with me. You interrupted class to ask for my name and number, in front of everyone.

You showed up for our date in **scrubs that you borrowed from your uncle**, despite not working in a hospital, because *"they are comfortable"*. It was embarrassing. Your brain damage was sadly *allegedly* a result of being beaten by cops. It must have negatively affected your emotions because when I replied, *"not much, you?"* to your *"what's up"* text message, you completely **flew off the handle** and cussed me out. You said some hurtful and scary things. It was unsettling. Sorry that I had to block you. **Thank you.**

Dear *"Big"* Theo:

The nickname you gave yourself for having *big*...shoulders because you once played Rugby. You lived far away from me, and we met at a job that required us to live away from home for a summer. When I tried to meet you at apparently the *"only coffee shop"* in your small town (*there were two, by the way*) and getting stuck in a **very backed up** highway along the way, you said that you could **no longer meet up with me** because you were *"painting with"* your dad...it was a very **long, slow, drive**. When this made me **lose interest**, you sent me flowers and love song lyrics to try and convince me to take you back (*roughly six months after we had stopped talking...*). It was simply not meant to be. **Thank you.**

Thank you, next.

To My Top Boys Part 2

Dear *Andre*:

We met one weekend at a live music show in *Small Town, Canada*. You seemed to have a good sense of humour at the time, but you then clung onto my friends and I, for the remainder of our trip. You even insisted on shadowing us to all the meals and shows that we attended (did you not have a home?). The real problem was, however, that every time you saw a piano in a public place (and there seemed to be one, in what felt like, every lobby and street corner that weekend), you would get all hyper and **had to run up to it and play it**, you explained to us that you could **never** leave a piano *unplayed*. You were a pretty good piano player (to my untrained ear), in spite of the fact that you claimed that you never had lessons, nor did you know how to read music. The entire weekend vibe was simply too intense for me. **Thank you.**

Dear *Ralph*:

I threw out a bunch of my dating rules and standards and decided to give you a shot. Most notably, would be seeing past the bad haircuts (you said that you have had the same hairstylist your entire life, and I imagine the same hairstyle), the fact that you still live with your parents **when pushing 40** (even going to festivals and sharing hotel rooms on weekend getaways together), or your squeaky voice **caused by poor dental hygiene** as a child. You came on a little strong with immediately calling me perfect (at least you got this right...***kidding***) and dropping the old "***I love you***" **bomb** ten minutes into our first conversation (you barely even knew me, never even asked me questions about myself), on top of the over **150 text messages** that I was waking up to daily, which wound up with me being forced to block you. Unfortunately for me, you did not get the hint and proceeded to **change your number roughly 16 times**, getting a new number every time, I blocked one (the cause of this was specifically because your *Mom* wanted to know why I was so ***flighty***). You eventually wore me down and I agreed to meet up with you. The meet up was fine, except for the fact that you took creepy photos of me from the rooftop of our meeting spot (how long did you spend standing there, waiting for me? More importantly, how did you know which route I would take?) However, when you went on to lecture me the next day by **nonstop text messages and voicemails**, for being unavailable to see again you so soon, I decided that it was time to stop playing nice and give up, blocking you once more. **Please do not change your number to try and contact me again. Thank you.**

Dear *Broke Benedict*:

You were always broke and needed to borrow cash, especially for gas for your car. I did lend you money that **one** time but notably you never gave me a ride anywhere (what did I actually pay for? ***You left the party without me...***). We lost touch for a number of years and when we did get back in touch one day, a lovely chat predictably became about needing gas money once more, as you revealed that you were **allegedly** and **coincidentally** stranded downtown. I said *"no"* and half an hour later you sent another lengthy text message beginning with *"**help me! I am desperate! I was just robbed!**"*. I ignored you and **you blocked me**. I hope that you were able to find your way home. **Thank you.**

Dear *Malcolm*:

You were a **colleague** who was always willing to help me with paperwork (during work hours, **obviously**) over our two years of working together. You always had a good sense humour too, making light out of any situation. When you were leaving the office for other job opportunities, the creepy text messages from you began. I assumed that they started due to a drunken stupor, but they continued. You must have read the *"Fifty Shades"* series because you would always ask if I wanted to meet for coffee and whenever I would say *"sure!"* the messages would always rapidly take a turn and become about how you were planning to hogtie and blindfold me and throw me into the trunk of your car, when you saw me... (what happened to a simple coffee? Is this not a kidnapping?). You were **two decades older** than me and I just **did not see you that way**. It made me uncomfortable, but I am sorry that I had to block you. **Thank you.**

Dear *Martin*:

14

In the reversal of *Malcolm* above, I agreed to help you with your paperwork, specifically the wording of professional emails. I was going through a brutal job hunt and thought that I could use the distraction. However, as soon as we finished drafting your emails, **you became relentless** in seeking my opinion for the wording in everything (you must have **somehow** managed before me). You drove me **insane** the way you called me constantly to ask for help, even when I told you that I was either busy preparing for interviews or other commitments. Whenever I did lend a hand, you never even said "*thank you*". I am sorry that you did not end up getting the response to the emails that you had initially wanted but it was all very overwhelming for me, especially considering that I was trying to figure my own stuff out too. I am sure your girlfriend could have provided her opinions on the emails for you. You could have even offered to pay somebody or at least offered to provide them a coffee. **Thank you.**

Dear *Stefan*:

We met up spontaneously for drinks one night. You were dressed sharply **in a suit and fedora**, however, you looked **much older** than your pictures and the age that you claimed to be (I really do not like being *Catfished!*). Apparently, the reason for the *fedora* was because you were *acting manager* at your workplace for the week, and you wanted to **look the part**. Though, this made me question what you actually did for work. You were good company, and I had a nice time, however, you claimed that you have **never** had a

15

passport or driver's license because you did not see the point of **leaving the City**, I envisioned a very boring life. **Thank you.**

Dear *Mark*:

I knew you for years and I used to think that you would be my "***end game***", should we ever date. After losing touch for a few years, we both attended the same *Bachelorette Party* for a mutual friend because you were considered as "*one of the girls*" (your words, not mine) and went to the wedding together. I had a really nice time with you as we danced the night away. After the wedding went so well, you **finally** asked me out on a date. ***Unfortunately***, you wanted **our first date** to be a home-cooked meal with your parents and sister (as you were still living at home), none of whom I had ever actually met before. I said that I was **uncomfortable** with this plan because it felt too soon. You stopped talking to me for the following week and when you finally decided to "***man up***" (again, your words) and tell me the problem, you explained that it was because you **assumed** that me not being ready to meet your parents, meant that I **must have *commitment issues***. You told our mutual friends what your problem was with me, **before even speaking to me** (during that week of silence) (***Tea* with the girls?**). I felt that was **embarrassing and unfair**, but regardless our friends chose to **keep you and cut me. Thank you.**

Thank you, next.

The Eligible Bachelors (...and why I blocked them)

Every year, during the summer season, people seem to try and pop back into my life that I have not spoken to, **or thought of**, in years. Now, when I say that, I am not talking about one *"what's up"* message after not talking for a few months, I mean they relentlessly reappear after vanishing for 6-10 years, **calling and messaging from different numbers and platforms**. I am not sure what it is about summer that makes people **obsessively** think of me. Before you go thinking that I am just cocky, I have the **receipts** (to my *Boomers*: by that I mean a few examples below).

The first, *Oliver,* I worked with for one summer, longer ago than I am willing to admit. He was a nice enough person who made the occasional effort to keep in touch, but I felt nothing romantic towards him. A few years after our job together, *Oliver* started dating *Sally* and eventually asked her to marry him (she said "yes").

After years of *Oliver* asking me to meet up and catch up, I finally agreed to attend a party with him and his friends (**"the Party"**). After all, I wanted to hear about the engagement and wedding. The *Party* took place **two weeks before *Oliver's* wedding**, and after a few too many drinks, **Oliver professed his love to me**. *Oliver* told me how different his life would have been, had I asked him

17

out on a date back when we worked together (why was that up to me though? Also, I did not see *Oliver* in this way). I found the whole thing **uncomfortable** and ended up **blocking him** on all the various media platforms. **I did not attend his wedding**.

Fast forward many years, summer rolled around, and I started receiving text messages from a random number. The person texting me would not reveal who they were, because they liked the idea of meeting for coffee *completely blindly* for me. This went on for days and eventually I got annoyed and threatened to block the number. He finally revealed himself to be a *very married* Oliver. Despite **the ring**, *Oliver* is still insisted on taking me out on a date. **Blocked.**

Oliver **still tries to pop back into my life every summer since, but I now recognize the number and tone of message and just block him straight away.**

Next up and sticking with the *random text theme*, was *Oliver's* friend, *Ryan*. I barely knew *Ryan*, having only met him one time, but he remembered me from *the Party*, though it is unclear how he got my number. That aside, it was someone else texting from a random number, it almost felt like *Oliver* and *Ryan* planned this together. *Ryan* also wanted to meet up blindly and reveal who it was in person. The random number shared a lot of details of their life story before I knew who they even were. They explained how that they had a traumatic brain injury, worked as a grocery store clerk, and still lived with their parents at the age of 40. It was a lot for me to take in considering that I had only met *Ryan* once. Me, not wanting to go through another round of this *"guess who this is"* exercise, demanded that he tell me who he was. *Ryan* then finally told me who it was, and I stopped responding to his messages and eventually **blocked him**. I really did not want to be part of *Oliver's* friend group anymore by this point, with the **love confessions** and date offers while married, and all.

The last of this infamous friend trilogy was *Daniel*. *Daniel* was Oliver's best friend. A few years prior to the infamous *Party*, *Oliver* had set *Daniel* and me up on an **uncomfortable blind date**. He did not dress well (wore his dad's very old-fashioned shirts from the **1970's disco era**) and did not look anything like the pictures from **10 years ago** that he had displayed on social media. In fact, when I went to the bathroom, he was completely shocked that I came back (I just did not have the arm strength to jump out the window). Nonetheless, we went out a few times, until *Daniel* dumped me because he was not ready for a relationship (who said that I was though?).

I saw *Daniel* at *the Party* and we still got along, despite his wardrobe still remaining the same.

A few years later, during summer of *course*, *Daniel* reached out, though, refreshingly enough, the number was not mysterious. We were both going through a *gym rat* phase at this point, and living *downtown*, though *Daniel negatively* considered

19

his *condominium* just a "*money pit*" and nothing more. We would check in and chat now and then, but *Daniel* always canceled any coffee plans and constantly criticized himself.

Daniel's neighbour had apparently fell victim to depression and jumped from the balcony and unfortunately did not survive. *Daniel* often spoke of this in great detail. *Daniel* wound up **blocking me** out of the blue. Later on, *Oliver* sent me a message to explain that *Daniel* had some sort of "*extreme depressive episode*" and attempted to harm himself. Thankfully, *Daniel* was able to get the help he needed before it was too late and ended up in some sort of live-in *facility*. I remain **blocked** and have not heard from *Daniel* since but sincerely wish him well.

Sticking with the random summer text theme, **our fourth** contender is *Zane*. I went out with *Zane* twice; he has a really inspiring childhood story of overcoming the odds of enduring multiple surgeries and being told he would never walk but becoming a martial art instructor in spite of this. I thought the inspiration might help me get into fitness myself and decided to meet up with him. *Zane* fell in love with me straight away (who wouldn't though?).

The first time we went out on a date, *Zane* tried to invite me on a weekend long skiing trip in *Small Town, Canada*, which was happening the next day. He wanted me to help him set up a surprise engagement for his friend and then spend the weekend together. **This was too much, too fast for me.**

The second time, when I revealed that I **may** want children **in the future**, *Zane* wrote me a long, unnecessary, and *frankly* unsettling message about various and lengthy health issues in his family, and about how children in his family are usually born without limbs. I believed him considering his childhood, but also who said I wanted children with him? **Blocked.**

Zane has never given up on another chance. **Every 6 months or so for over seven years**, he finds another way to contact me. *Zane* usually reaches out to reiterate and explain that he was lying about his family medical history, though, most recently he contacted me to show pictures of his puppy (much like a stranger trying to kidnap you would). **I never respond.**

Finally, there is *Clarence*, who *coincidentally*, just called me again as I write this *post*, from yet another **different number.**

Clarence is very tall and apparently owns his own business doing *Court* related typing tasks and **allegedly** lives in both the *U.S.A.* and *the City* (which does not make sense to me for a slew of reasons...including the fact that both countries would have different legal systems...but anyway.). **We went out twice.** Both times, *Clarence* suggested a bar and then would not eat or drink, which made me uncomfortable (I mean, why not suggest coffee or a movie then?).

21

The second date, *Clarence* tried to talk me into going **back to his place,** I was not feeling it and refused. I did not hear from him again. **Over six years later**, once more in the summertime, I received a text from yet another random number. *Clarence* told me that he was coming back to *the City* for the summer and that he really wanted to get together because he enjoyed my company. At first, he made a *"joke"* about having *"unfinished business"* from our last encounter. I took offence and **blocked him.** Over a week later, *Clarence* texted me, this time from his **work number** to apologize and once again attempted to request my presence during his *City* visit. I decided that the whole thing was a waste of my time. **Blocked again.**

So, tell me, *Dear Journal,* why do these guys disappear for literally years and then become relentless about wanting my company, messaging me from all sorts of numbers every time I block them? Why do they always assume that I am single? Do I need to change my 20-year long number for real (I often threaten to for the sake of a fresh start but I really do not want to)? Finally, do any of the guys entice you, shall I pass along your number? Let me know.

Part 2
Friendships in The City

Hot Girl Summer (Part 1/3)

Many moons ago, I managed to get back in touch with some people that I knew in elementary school, they all went to high school together and remained friends ("**the Group**"). I was in contact with them [thanks to social media] but I was not a member of the *Group*. I figured that spending my time with them would be less drama for my life [I was wrong], since they had known me for years, we had similar upbringings, and I simply thought that they would just generally know what would upset me [they did not care].

I bonded fast with this one girl in particular, *Kim* (*the "Model"*), she noticed that I had lost weight and suddenly started inviting me to various clubs and parties. She went to high school with the *Group,* and we would both attend the same reunions. I had known her for a few years at this point, but we had just never bonded [I had always thought she was a bit stuck up].

It was nice to be invited out. *Kim*, unfortunately, did not have a job though [and apparently *"runway models"*, who sit around at home, do not make much money...] so it was almost always me paying for everything, [including her cigarettes, *when I did not even smoke* (in fact, I am allergic to tobacco), and for her taxis because **she refused to take** the local transit...], which I really did not have a problem with since I was working full time and therefore had a regular income [and no rent to pay].

[Kim had family problems or boy problems almost *daily*, this would require us to meet up **almost every night** so that she could smoke (*a pack a night*), drink (*double Gin and soda and keep them coming*) and vent, even if I was not feeling well. She would always say that I was the only one who she could truly count on to be there for her and so I felt a **constant pressure** to physically be there.]

Everything was pretty much fine and dandy until around the *Canada's Day* long weekend. *Janice* [who was *Kim*'s "*best friend*", until I came into the picture], had a house party to celebrate the long weekend. At this point, I was basically convinced that *Janice* **did not like me** [even though I was her **first friend** in Canada] because *Kim* and I were spending so much time together, and *jealousy* is a terrible emotion.

I did not want to go to this party, mainly because their parties always involved drinking, smoking and listening to their high school stories [or watching the same old videos that they took in high school, *over and over again*], and I just do not do well sitting and drinking [I do love dancing though], I do not smoke, and I do not do well **drinking when bored**, basically I was afraid that I would **end up drunk**. *Kim* got pushy about me going because she wanted *Janice* and I to "*bond better*" [or so she said, I think she had just wanted me to do the cigarette and liquor run], but after much convincing, I ended up going [and of course, I had to do said item pick up].

There were two new guys there, who happened to be visiting from Ireland and were staying with a friend of *Janice*'s [both guys were named *Liam*] ("**the Liams**"), and I spent a lot of time chatting with them, since I had only just arrived back from a trip to Ireland. We were playing cards and discussing the Irish clubs that I had gone to, which I certainly found more interesting than watching those high school videos for the *90th time*. Suddenly, out of nowhere, *Janice's* friend *Valerie* [who was a few years older than the rest of us and acted as *Janice's* bodyguard], came up to me and told me to get into her car, as she was going to take me home.

I was **a bit *intoxicated*** and was going to be chain-locked out of my house [since I was supposed to stay over like everyone else had planned to]. I could not understand why I was the *only one* getting kicked out. I argued with *Janice,* and she said there was no room for me to stay [but room for everyone else]. I asked *Kim* [who had literally just spilled red wine all over the white carpet, in her *drunken stupor*], if she had anything to say, or if she was going to leave with me, and she responded "*no*" to both questions.

After that party, I stopped getting invited to places because apparently the *Liams* did not like me. Everyone else, including *Kim*, were going to these events and parties, just not me. I was still lending *Kim* the cash to go because *Janice* had previously made a comment about *Kim* being a **freeloader** and *Kim* (*ironically*) wanted to **prove her wrong**. No one understood how **frustrating** this was for me, so after a while I gave up on asking why I was not invited.

One day, a few months later, *Kim* and I were supposed to meet up. She completely disappeared. It had turned out that it was all because she went to another BBQ hosted by the *Liams* [it is still unclear who bought her drinks and cigarettes for this BBQ]. I felt as if she probably could have just cancelled the plans with me, instead of disappearing. She could not understand why I was annoyed, and I found it annoying that she did not understand. It turned into a **huge stupid fight**. She eventually decided that we **could not** be friends until I worked on my *issues* and had a *better self-esteem*. Apparently, the entire *Group* had a whole discussion, roughly a month earlier, in a public restaurant I might add [that I obviously provided the money for *Kim* to attend], that until I was more confident and had no more *personal issues*, no one wanted anything to do with me.

[It is still unclear why they thought kicking me out of the *Group* would help...and to this day I am so embarrassed that they had all discussed this without me being there to *defend myself*].

[Also, I may have some *issues*, but I was not the one borrowing money to drink...]

I found out maybe a year later that apparently, the original plan was that *Janice* was eventually going to invite me out for coffee to discuss said *issues* and maybe consider letting me back into the *Group*, when she felt that I was ready. This never happened [I guess I was never ready]. I have not heard from *Janice* since.

The **most *awkward*** part in all of this was, both *Kim* and another person from the *Group*, *Sally* [who I knew since I was about 7 years old], attended the same *College* as I did. One day, when I bumped into both of them in the College library, I made the mistake of being too friendly [commented on the weather or something] and was asked by *Sally* to leave...and although *Kim* had never been rude to me in person [at this point, anyway], *Sally* has always given me attitude for reasons unknown.

[*Sally* is about *four feet tall*, and what she lacks in height, she makes up for in *width*. *She acts as Kim's protector* (she used to tell me that this was because *Kim* "*is (her) girl*") ....it is just a little funny to me considering *Kim* is tall (5'11) and is being '*protected*' by someone so short (although, *Sally* could probably take me)].

I considered *Kim* to be my best friend. I have lent her a ridiculous amount of money, **on the understanding that I would get it back once she had a job** [I never got it back]. I thought of her like a *sister,* and I would have been there for her through anything, I was fiercely loyal, much like *Sally*. I used to think that *Kim* and the *Group* would be there for me too [I have not been invited to a reunion since...] I think they probably would have been if *jealousy* had not reared its ugly head. The

28

funny part is, I think that because I am all of their common enemy, the whole *Group* became closer. **Hating me brought them love.**

This probably would have been a nice ending if I did not go through **this two more times...**

To   *be*   *continued...*

Hot Girl Summer (Part 2/3)

After surviving my first round of drama with *Kim* and the *Group*, life marched on (*as it always does*). I was able to save some money, I enrolled in a *College* night school program to work towards a second diploma, and I spent the weekends with my *College friends*. I was doing well.

One weekend, when I was out with my *College* friends, *Kim* and *Sally* walked into the same bar that we were at. I ignored them completely and **it felt amazing**. However, a few days later, *Kim* sent me a text message (*I nearly dropped my phone when her name popped up*). She asked me if we could meet up later in the week, as she had some items to return to me. Against my better judgment, I eventually agreed.

When I saw her, she told me that she had a **disastrous birthday party**, a few months earlier. It was a hotel party, in which she had tried to introduce her new boyfriend, *Terrence*, to the *Group*. Apparently, the fact that he was also going to stay in the same hotel room as the *Group*, made everyone uncomfortable and the *Group* left the hotel room to go to their respective homes. *Janice* kicked *Kim* out of the *Group*, as punishment.

On top of this, *Kim* was having issues with her **super religious parents**. Her *father* **allegedly** pushed her down the **concrete stairs** in their garage, after she

arrived *home drunk* one night. As a result, she twisted her ankle and was unable to wear **her new birthday heels** for months. These events all made her realize that I *would have been there* for her and that is why she reached out. However, it should be noted, that she did ask for separate bills at our reunion. I felt that, after everything, she should have just covered me, but it was a **gesture, nonetheless.**

Kim was still attending the same *College* as me. My classes did not start until the evening, as I was working fulltime during the day, but apparently *Kim* was *"in charge"* of, and *"staring in"* a fashion night at the *College*, so she was often still there when I would arrive for my class. She told me that she was no longer eating, just smoking instead to curb her appetite, and honestly, she looked *unhealthy*, so when I would pick up my dinner on my way to class, I would sometimes pick her up something to eat too, out of concern. **It begins again...**

She invited me one weekend to a *"house party"*, to meet *Terrence* and his *"rock star"* friends. When I arrived at this party, I discovered that *Terrence* was over **twenty years older** than us, five feet tall, **married**, wore make-up better applied than I could ever achieve, and had **kids that were in our age group**. He was also a starving artist, with a love for fashion, trying to make it in the music industry. Suddenly, the fact that nobody wanted to stay overnight at the birthday hotel party, made a lot of sense. I then learned that when *Kim* first introduced *Terrence* to the *Group*, she told them that he was her *"gay friend"*. They did not realize any differently until *Terrence* and *Kim* started making out on the hotel bed, although *Kim* assured me that she thought that everyone knew that she was joking about the "*gay*" thing. [Why would they think that she was joking though?]

Following this party, *Kim* spent the night with *Terrence*, and apparently, when she arrived back at her house the next morning, her mother was inconsolable and revealed to *Kim* that she "*had a vision in prayer circle*", that *Kim* was dating a **married man**. She also saw them making out in his car in their driveway, moments earlier. *Kim*'s parents told her to either move out, or break-up with *Terrence*. So, *Kim* moved to **Small Town, Canada,** to live with her previously banished sister, *Betty*, another **starving artist**.

The reason that *Kim* had any money whatsoever beforehand to pay for separate bills on our nights out, was because she was working part-time for her *father*'s business. With this move to *Small Town*, it meant that **she would no longer have that income**.

Betty is 10 years older than *Kim* [their brother, *Dan*, is 8 years older than *Kim*, so *Kim* always considered her conception to be a **mistake**]. *Betty* had four children and each child had a different father. Her parents had full custody of the older two children [who were a result of two teenage pregnancies], and the other children lived with *Betty*. *Betty* was trying to **get discovered** as a singer and **make it big**, so she spent her evenings performing at a bar (*which seemed to be the common occupation in*

Small Town). She **did not have** a fulltime job. She was also an alcoholic who dabbled in various drugs.

The benefit of *Kim* living with her sister, was that *Terrence* could now drop by and see her before his gigs, which usually took place in *Small Town*. They would then get ready and head to whichever bar that he was performing at that night. It was all well and good except, *Kim* had no money and could not get a job because *Betty* relied on her to babysit during the day [instead of *Kim* paying *Betty* for rent or groceries]. *Terrence* could not use cash or credit cards **without his wife noticing**, as they were her cards. *Betty* used whatever little money she made from her gigs for her kids, or for her various vices. That is where I came in. I was once again consumed by this life and the drama it consisted of, and I, once again, felt a constant pressure to visit *Kim* and *"be there for her"*. I felt especially bad that she no longer had the *Group*, she only had me.

She *(predictably)* would always need me to drop off the usual alcohol and cigarettes', but she now had a new request of me lending her cash to tide her over until my next visit [usually, she would ask for $300]. Sometimes, *Betty* would allegedly find the cash that I would lend to *Kim* **and keep it**, so my next visit would then have to happen sooner than I planned.

Eventually, a few weeks later, *Kim's* parents bought her a car (*that I never saw*) to convince her to move back home (*although, she did not have a driver's license*), and she did. However, they took away her cellphone, upon her arrival, as a punishment for leaving, and she would now have to sleep in the car if she arrived home after midnight. Therefore, *Terrence* now had to text me to **pass along messages** to *Kim*, as it was too nerve wracking for him to call her parents' house phone. At first it was fine, I actually liked talking to someone so much older, who had been through the drama before, but it got awkward **real quick**.

One instance was when we went to a party that a guy, **who I happened to be interested in**, invited us to. *Terrence* kept texting me to ask for a *play-by-play* on what *Kim* was doing and what was happening, I would respond, thinking that it would put his anxiety at ease, however, he then got really angry at me when I eventually stopped responding. I was not trying to ignore him; I had put my phone away to try and focus on said guy.

Terrence also proposed to *Kim*, **on my birthday**, via text message **on my phone** [*Kim* said "yes", but I mean, not only was *Terrence* still married, but he was also still living with his wife...]. The focus of my birthday was now on the proposal, nonetheless.

The three of us went to a party, later in the summer, I had to cover myself and the both of them. Things were awkward this night, especially since *Terrence* was giving me the **silent treatment**, as I had told him earlier that week that I was not going to be his "*eye and ears*" anymore. It was too weird to be ratting out my "*best friend*". I got frustrated, once again, about feeling used and honestly tired of being the *messenger*. [When did everyone become my responsibility??] I was developing a lot of built-up anger and resentment. I was tired of having a fulltime job and nothing to show for it because of all these cash donations. I was tired of struggling. I was tired of always having to apologize for not watching *Kim* closely enough or for not giving a detailed enough *"play-by-play"*. I was mostly tired of everything feeling like it was always my fault. I started being very vocal at this party. I mean, *Terrence* was over **20 years older than us**...I would hope that he could cover the bill or at least cover the portion for himself and/or *Kim*, I was quite adamant that I would only be paying for myself at this party.

Terrence gave me a ride home from this party, which I did not want, but felt pressure from all directions to take. During the ride, *Terrence* felt that I was being rude about my **financial troubles,** and he felt that I was being **disrespectful** to *Kim* (*what about my feelings though?*), he pulled over on the busiest highway of *the City* and said that I had to get out and walk. Although, he changed his mind when I threatened to call the police and report him for his *drinking and driving*, although he did not appear drunk, I was sure that he would *"blow over"*. I also pointed out that it was like a 25KM walk along the highway and that I would likely be killed (*I do not think he cared about this though*). Apparently, after nearly killing me and then dropping me off at home, *Kim* and *Terrence* headed to *Kim's father's* office, *to make love*, and work out the **frustrations caused by me**. *Kim's* *father's* office was often her secret location for a late-night *rendezvous* [which I always thought was a little disrespectful].

Meanwhile, *Kim* was distancing herself from me once again, she only really wanted to see me if *Terrence* was in town or when I received my paycheque. I would agree to these meetups because I did not want all the effort that I made to be there for her that summer, and supporting everyone else in the process, to be for nothing. *Janice* had apparently allowed *Kim* back into the *Group* and she could now attend their parties once more, which I still was **not allowed to attend**, though usually secretly funded them.

One day, *Kim* and I met for a drink, to try and talk things out. Within **ten minutes** of the drinks arriving, she chugged her drink, left her *maxed out credit card* on the table and, apparently, went outside for a cigarette but completely **disappeared**. I was stuck with a *useless credit card* and another bill to cover. She still had no cellphone, so when I tried to call her parent's house phone, to see if she arrived home safely and if she wanted **her credit card back**, her *father* told me to "*take a hint*" and to never call that number again. Her *mother* also insisted on speaking to me and called me "*the blonde devil*" [I thought this was a rather **sexy** nickname] and said that I was "*the blind leading the blind*", though I am quite sure that this was, in fact, the other way around. (*What do I do with the credit card though?*)

I was confused and had never been ditched at a bar like that before. Nor had I ever been stuck with someone else's credit card. I mean, I genuinely thought that something terrible had happened to her, until I spoke with her parents and assumed that she was probably alright. I was upset with myself for **tolerating being used** for what was now, two summers, but I was also relieved. I was tired of *Terrence* and the **constant pressure** of helping *Kim*. So, I mailed her shredded credit card to her home address, and I did my best to keep moving forward.

To be continued...

Hot Girl Summer (Part 3/3)

I know what you are all thinking – **how is there possibly a third part?** I ask myself that same question.

Shorty after losing touch with *Kim* for the second time, I managed to get a new job. The job had more potential for growth, however, I only survived there for **six weeks**. I lost this job in *December*, which made it even harder with the *Holiday Season*, and it was the first time that I had ever been let go from a job. This got me thinking that, now that the *tables were turned* and I was the unemployed one, maybe if *Kim* now had a job, it would be her covering me. (*Naïve*, I know.)

I spent a few weeks job hunting and eventually I managed to get a job with a higher pay (it was actually the first and only job that paid me a higher salary than I asked for) and a better benefits package. It was a one-year maternity leave position, with the potential to stay on longer.

Shortly after receiving that new job position, I coincidentally received a text message from *Kim*, she had seen my winning article in our *College* paper, and she wanted to meet up and talk.

It started out the same old way. An apology. Drama that made *Kim* appreciate me, (she and *Terrence* had since broken up. *Terrence* had **predictably** chosen his wife over *Kim*), family issues, *Group* issues and, obviously, she was broke and it was back to me covering the bar tabs. The thought remained in the back of my mind that if the tables were reversed, **she would be there for me**.

One weekend, we went to a party hosted by my event planning cousin, *Jonathan*. For my entire life up until this point, I had always thought that *Jonathan* was the **coolest guy**. He was quite a number of years older than me and had spent his entire career as an *event planner* for *college students* and he was always on top of the latest trends and music.

At the end of this party, when I went to pay my tab, the *Club* revealed that they would only take cash and there was no *ATM* inside the *Club*. I offered to go find an *ATM* and come back to pay for the bill, but *Jonathan* came waltzing over and kindly covered it. I bought him a late-night meal and I paid him back the cash as soon as we found an *ATM* that night, though when *Jonathan* **reported this back to my parents**....he conveniently left that part out.

After *Jonathan* met *Kim*, he found her on social media and started sending her messages (*slid into her DMs*). He claimed that after a few messages, he was hooked and loved her, without ever going out on a date or having a real chance to speak in person. He would send her videos of his closet so that she can pick out his outfit of the day. He sent her photos of his fresh manicures and clean shoes. He told her all about his parents (my *aunt* and *uncle*) and his fears for the future. He even asked her questions about me. After everything that had happened between *Kim* and I, **I hated this**. Especially when I found out that he was asking about me (I mean, he had already ***reported back to my parents*** about me, less than a month earlier). Whenever I asked *Jonathan* to stop, he would tell me that it was too late, he was already *in love*. Whenever I asked *Kim* to stop, she made me feel *irrational*.

Whenever *Kim* and I would hit up *the City* and if *Jonathan* knew where we were, he would offer to come pick *Kim* up and give her a ride back to his place. No ride for me though, because *Jonathan* figured that I could "*find (my) own way home*" (even though my home was only **ten minutes** out of his way). *Kim*, thankfully, never took him up on this (to my knowledge, anyway).

Meanwhile, life for me was rapidly **going downhill**. That sweet new job that I had, ***did not work out*** because the baby was tragically **a stillborn** and there was no longer a way to justify my one-year contract.

In the span of **three months: I broke three toes**, had a **bad bruise on my knee bone**, causing it to swell up like a balloon and making it excruciating to walk (I was convinced it was broken at one point), a **broken nose**, **I lost my job**, and **I was broke**. I was in ***a low place*** and on top of this, I had to hear about how my cousin was constantly messaging my "*best friend*" and calling her every day at 5:00 p.m.

40

I tried reaching out to *Jonathan* and reveal everything that was going on with me, but he basically just called me **dramatic** and said that he *"does not like to hear drama"* and continued this online relationship with *Kim*. Blood was **not** thicker than water.

When *Kim* and *Jonathan* finally did go out on their date, they watched a movie and then *Jonathan* basically had his **one-night stand** and **never called Kim again**. After all of that and I was stuck having to pick up the pieces and explain why my cousin, who was once **obsessed** with her, was no longer calling her. I heard through the *family grapevine* that *Jonathan* had decided that *Kim* was too immature for him (based on some story that *Kim* had told him about driving without a driver's license). *Kim* did try coming over to my parents' house during a family holiday party, I think to try and confront *Jonathan*, though I sent her away in order to avoid the inevitable *angry lecture* in front of everyone. We did see *Jonathan* at another *college party*, for a **final time**, a few months later. He was all over *Kim* on the dancefloor, despite now having a serious girlfriend.

Meanwhile, I was still working at the occasional temporary job. *Kim* managed to get a fulltime job, but it was a commissioned based, *door-to-door job*. Whenever she had money, she would go out with her coworkers but not with me, she would bring *Sally* to these events instead. Whenever I had money, guess who was at my door? (Not with *Sally* though. By this point, *Sally* had told me to *"do the world a favour and jump off a bridge*"...again, I do not know what her problem with me was...)

When I finally did get a permanent work position, *Kim* coincidentally decided to quit her *door-to-door* job in order to "*focus on modeling*". As a result, *Kim* would be waiting in my workplace lobby every time that I got paid, or if I did not want to meet up, she would call my office number with some outrageous drama (*e.g.* her mom would occasionally *(allegedly)* call the police on her, coincidentally, always on my pay day) and so she would have to take a taxi and wait outside for me to come down to the lobby with cash to pay for the cab.

We had a friend who was a regular at a *Bar* near my new workplace. Apparently one day, on a non-pay week (for me), *Kim*, *Sally*, and this friend, spent the day drinking and making fun of me, with the bar staff. After this, I always cringed a little when I went to this *Bar* with my new colleagues, dreading what the staff would tell my coworkers about me.

One time, I was meeting a blind date at that same *Bar* and *Kim* waited for him with me. He ordered a beer and disappeared; I thought that maybe he went to the bathroom. *Kim apparently* saw him outside, when she was having a smoke, and he *allegedly* told her that he was leaving the *Bar* because he did not realize that I had an **unattractive face.**

42

It was at a point where I was **always incredibly enraged**. I was so sick of always being the *"bad guy"* and the less attractive friend, despite consistently trying my best and always struggling to find a way to make money. No matter what would happen, *Kim* was always the **victim,** and everyone **would believe her** and hate me, including my own cousin, who knew me *my entire life*.

One night, after nearly a year of this (normally this friendship would last one summer and then I would have my *winter mental health break*) we went out for a drink, and I realized that some cash I had hidden in a secret spot in my purse **was gone.** *Kim* was the only one who knew where the cash was and she was the only one anywhere near my purse (and this was not the first time that my cash had gone missing), so this fight between us was particularly bad. *Kim* ended up leaving (once again, without saying a word) and received a ride home from some *guy* at the bar (I saw them drive by when they left). The *guy's* friend informed me that he had overheard the conversation and that *Kim's* car ride was in exchange of sexual favours (he offered me the same deal, but I said *no,* the **10-minute car ride** was probably not worth it). **I never heard from her again.**

I think *Jonathan* and *Kim* likely kept in touch for a while over social media, but I do not know if she and *Sally* still attended his events, although I would not be surprised as *Sally* once called *Jonathan* *"easy on the eyes"*. (What can I say? I come from good genes.)

I did not talk to *Jonathan* **for years** after this, I would simply ignore him at family parties. To this day he has never apologized to me, but I have reluctantly apologized to him (as an attempt to *"keep the peace"*). He is **no longer** the ***cool cousin*** in my eyes, nor will I ever introduce him to any of my friends again. We only really started slightly speaking again recently, after the birth of his ***beautiful daughter***, and I hope that he is someone that she can always rely on to be there for her (even if that means drama).

It took me a long time to get over this. My *self-esteem* and *self-worth* were in the gutter. Working for a terrible boss very shortly after all of this, forced me into self-improvement. I think the reason that I let this *'friendship'* go on for so long and take so much out of me, was because after all of the ***money, time, energy, and effort*** that I put into it, I do not think that I could handle it being **all for nothing**. I think that I was hopeful that maybe I could ***teach Kim some empathy*** and help her become a better person. All that I ended up getting was ***debt, broken bones, an inability to go to any elementary school reunion (thanks Janice), a lost cousin, and a bad reputation***.

I think that the **saddest part** of all of this, is that something that felt so significant in my life (at the time), did not make a difference in *Kim's* life at all. I think that I was likely just replaced with someone else to cover her bar tabs and she moved on without a second thought about me and without any sort of consequence. I used to think that one day we could finally meet up and I could get

closure and maybe it would have shown me that it was not **all for nothing** but, realistically, I think that I would be **sucked right back in.**

I used to want to write an inspiring book for young adults, an *"it gets better"* type book or *"you can't buy friendship"*, but I keep waiting for my really inspiring ending *"and then I won the lottery and good karma came my way"*, or *"then I gave birth to genius identical triplets, who cured cancer"* type ending. My life just went on. I paid off my debt and now have a *"very good"* credit score, which is an accomplishment in itself. I have grown in my career, and I no longer struggle to hold onto a job, I have not had to work temporary jobs in years. *I pay my bills; I pay rent on time; I have my* *own sweet little apartment; I buy groceries that* *include more than just alcohol and party foods.* Best of all, I no longer pay anyone to stay in my life. My inspiring ending is an **average life**, with nice, loyal, people in it and I think that is probably **good enough**. Though, if a lottery win does come my way, **I will not object it.**

So, to those who are struggling or hitting their rock bottom, just keep moving forward. Do what makes you happy. Do what will be positive for you. It may be terrible for a while, but it does eventually get better, and never hesitate to reach out for help if you ever need it.

Rita

I first met *Rita* in *High School*. In fact, because of my decision of wanting a fresh start, *Rita* was my first friend in *High School*. We met in our very first class because the lockers were assigned alphabetically.

Rita was one of ten children (with three of the siblings being younger than her) and had a bit of a difficult upbringing but she was always determined to make a better life for herself, I found this to be admirable. She was the **first** in her family to go to *College*, the **first** of our group to get married at the **ripe old age of 20** and was the **first** to separate from her husband, when she met and fell in love with *Phil*, who was her colleague at the time and was going through a marriage separation himself. Despite the scandalous start, at the beginning, I thought that *Phil* was **great** for *Rita*, he was independent, friendly, a lot of fun and he was teaching *Rita* how to get out of debt. *Phil* even took *Rita* on her very first plane ride and beach vacation. However, **in my humble opinion**, it appeared that at some point in helping *Rita*, *Phil* took it to another level and became **controlling with everything**, or maybe there were always signs of this behaviour and I was just too **young and naïve** to notice. Regardless, right from the start, *Rita* would not go anywhere without *Phil*, and she lost a lot of friends because of this.

Tragically, *Rita's* youngest brother was shot and killed, while walking home from a nearby *Subway Station*. This horrendous situation made Rita determined to find a way to help her next youngest brother, *Calvin*, and his five-year-old daughter, get out of the neighbourhood, in hopes of keeping him safe. As *Calvin* did not have a job, *Rita* (obviously) thought that I should move in too, so that we could divide rent, groceries, and all other costs, into three and therefore save money (save money at whose expense though?).

We spent some time looking at various advertisements and houses. *Rita* and *Phil* needed a basement for their *vape juice* business, and they required rent cheaper than what they were currently paying, so that they could start saving for a down payment towards buying their own house. *Rita*, *Phil* and *Calvin*, also needed a yard for their various pets and *Calvin's* daughter to run around in. Therefore, all the houses that we were looking at were at least a **45-minute drive** (without traffic) into *the City* (I was already living downtown by this point). The thought was that we would carpool (with *Phil* being the driver) to and from work and ***then divide gas and car payments into three***.

The house that they were all most interested in (it was all a bit far from *the City* for my **bougie taste**), was very isolated (I mean – I would have really had to rely on *Phil* and their car) and the room that would have been for me, was tiny – maybe big enough for single bed with no furniture, had **no closet** and had **no window** (at least there's a door?) but it had access to the *Attic* (by that I mean, a space in the ceiling that I could stick my hand in, not an actual room) (you want me to pay 1/3 rent for this??). Most troubling, I was told that I would have to hide any cash away (by reaching up and sliding it into the *Attic*, I suppose) because *Calvin*'s daughter had a habit of pickpocketing. **The bonus part** of the plan was that *Phil* wanted to be in charge of my budget (I guess that I would just sign my paycheques over and get an allowance?) and it was important to *Rita* that the house be a safe place for the **hundreds** of other family members to crash at (sounds crowded...where do I fit into all of this?). **I was just in a different place in my life.**

After spending some time with *Phil*, I decided that I could not imagine living with him and keep my *mental health* in check. Unfortunately, *for me*, even though we put in a lower rent offer, **it was accepted.** All we had to do was pay first month's rent, last month's rent, and a security deposit, and the house would be ours. *Phil* also required a **two-year commitment from me** (most leases are only one year), so that he and *Rita* could save enough money for a down payment (according to *Phil*'s math calculations).

I really wanted to be there for *Rita*. She was my oldest friend and somebody that I could rely on to be there for me. She was also somebody that I had experienced all moments of *adulthood* with. I really wanted to support *Rita*, especially after her brother's sudden and tragic death. However, I just could not imagine **two years** of hiding my cash in a windowless room, *tiptoeing* around *Phil* while trying to **earn my allowance**, and being unable to go anywhere without a car (what about my dating life though? Would that have been in *Phil's* budget? Most importantly, would *Phil* have been my *chaperone* on these dates??). I also could not imagine ever really being able to move out, especially after *Rita* and *Phil* were used to two years of my financial contributions, I think I would have had to buy a house with them and become a **sister-wife**. **I had to choose me,** and this was not what I thought would be best and sadly, I lost my friend as a result.

Apparently, and as something that (**selfishly**) made me feel less guilty, *Calvin* decided that he was also **uncomfortable** with the whole thing and backed out as well. *Rita* and *Phil* lived in the house for a year and then found an apartment unit to rent, that was cheaper than what their rent had been before this journey had begun. I, **unfortunately**, never really hear from *Rita* anymore, I used to receive the occasional text message, but I think *Phil* must have found out that she was corresponding with me and put an end to that. However, I did receive a message from *Rita* not too long ago to inform me that *Phil* had fallen ill with some sort of rare disease (hopefully not from the homemade vape juice) and that they were collecting money for treatment (which was apparently costing them $20,000 a month – which is a lot, considering the **free Healthcare** in *Canada*) and I think that it was strongly implied that **I should offer to help** (I did not). Regardless, it sounded to me like they, **_unfortunately_**, were never able to save enough for that down payment.

In conclusion, and as a _lessons learned_, (and something that I am writing to remind myself), sometimes you just need to learn to let go of people, regardless of the history. After all, you cannot edit completed chapters, but you can start new ones.

Rita and Ivan

Long before Rita met *Phil* there was *Ivan*. *Ivan* was a few years older than us and friends with *Rita*'s brother. He was a shy, tall, and lanky fellow, but always seemed kind. *Rita*'s brother was initially annoyed when *Ivan* started going to their house for *Rita* instead of him, but they dated all through *High School*, nonetheless.

About five years into the relationship, *Rita*'s father's health was **rapidly declining,** and *Rita* decided that she wanted to get married while her father was still alive. I was thrilled to get invited; it was my **first non-family wedding**.

They rented a banquet hall for both the ceremony and wedding, and it was a **potluck style** wedding. All their friends and family provided the alcohol and the food.

Rita's father, who was now in a wheelchair, **got out of his chair to walk *Rita* down the aisle**, and *there was not a dry eye in sight.*

The bride was beautiful. The groom was handsome. The food was **excellent**, the cake was chocolate and **divine**, and I wrestled and **won that bouquet**, no wedding for me yet but same for anyone else who was after the bouquet (I must still be next). The night concluded with *Rita*'s cute little nieces singing karaoke.

A few months later, after *Rita* and *Ivan* had settled into married life, I met up with *Rita*. It turned out that after a challenging first few weeks of marriage, where they were living with *Ivan's* mother and stepfather, and *having to sit in silence in the bedroom* because *Ivan's* stepfather *hated the slightest sound*, *Rita*, *Ivan*, and *Ivan's* mother all moved into a two-bedroom apartment. The rent and all the other expenses were **solely Rita's responsibility,** as she was the only one with regular employment. On top of this, *Rita* was being relocated at work and she found this idea very stressful. *Rita* **was miserable but also felt trapped.**

It turned out that the *work relocation* was the **best thing** for *Rita*, *in her opinion*, because she met *Phil*, who was fiercely independent and self-sufficient. *Phil* would often let *Rita* "**crash**" at his place after an overnight shift, which used to worry *Ivan*. It later turned out that *Ivan* was **right to worry** as this "*crashing*" **evolved to love**.

The more time that *Rita* spent with *Phil*, the more she **resented *Ivan*** and his mother. *Rita* **especially hated** that if she asked *Ivan* to do something while she was at work, such as laundry, she would come home to find that his mother had done it instead. *Rita* really wanted to give their marriage at least a year as a fair shot, but as the one-year mark rapidly approached, *Rita* realized that she was ready to move on.

I went to the apartment unit to help *Rita* move some of her things to *Phil's* place and although *Ivan* was not home, his mother was. It was

horrendous as his mother was chasing us in tears, asking *Rita* to give *Ivan* another chance. **Rita never looked back.**

Rita lost a lot of friends **over this affair,** but she had *Phil* and, *as far as I could tell*, that was enough. However, all these years later (more than I am willing to admit), *Rita* and *Ivan* are still **technically married**. Neither are willing to **pay for a divorce** and, although I am sure that *Rita* would love to marry *Phil* one day, she is happy with what they have.

Christine

Longer ago than I am willing to admit, before the days of lockdown, mask mandates, vaccine passports, truck rallies and the current devastation in the *Ukraine*, I was a young teen beginning my *High School* journey. When I attended my very first *High School* class before lockers were even assigned, I was looking around to see my new classmates and spotted *Christine,* with her *highlighter-yellow-coloured* hair. *Rita* went marching into class shortly afterwards and **kicked Christine out of her seat** because she liked that seat better. I thought that *Rita* seemed like a **bully**, and that is how I spotted my first *High School* crew.

It turned out that *Rita* and *Christine* had been best friends since the fifth grade and the three of us became fast friends. Though, I was often made fun of by them for having pressed shirts, getting good grades, and being generally clumsy, but I would laugh it off.

I remember our first sleepover party at *Christine's* house and meeting her family, who were all very friendly, but a little strange (in my teenage mind). *Christine* had two younger brothers, one who sadly had a stroke when he was born and was **mentally delayed** as a result, and the other who would later be diagnosed as having *Schizophrenia* as an adult, after a severe mental episode.

Her mother was overweight, and had stopped walking and working, as a result. She would just lay on the couch all day, watching her *Soap Operas*. (In retrospect, it's goals!). She did not even stand up to say "*hi*" to me. Christine's dad, who worked in **HVAC repairs**, was the most interesting of them all. He had made the decision shortly after I met him, that he was going to stop brushing his teeth and **let them fall out** because he had a friend at the *Morgue* who could hook him up with **second-hand dentures for free**. He felt that brushing one's teeth was a "*waste of time*". He also did not shower much, he would often let the water run while reading his book, to take a break from everyone.

I remember once, I invited *Christine* and *Rita* to come to my house to go biking and swim at a nearby swimming pool. When *Christine's father* came to pick them both up, he was walking up and down my street **hollering Christine's name at the top of his lungs** because he could not remember the house number. We eventually heard him from inside the house and I thought it was quite embarrassing.

Christine was allowed to call her parents by their first names and scream and swear at both. Her parents had decided that because *Christine* was now in *High School* and therefore "*grown up*", they could now be "*adult friends*". I tried pushing this on my parents too, but they sadly never went for it, even to this day.

After *Grade 9*, I did not see *Christine* as often, as I had switched all my classes to the most challenging level and *Christine* and *Rita* stayed at the same level. I would still have some classes with *Rita* and get invited to the occasional party at *Christine's* house, but these parties were always a bit weird. *Christine's* friends now consisted of:

- **a girl who was unable to talk out loud** because she was "too *shy*". Her mother therefore went everywhere with her (including the parties), and she would whisper in her mother's ear whenever she had something to say, and her mother would then repeat it out loud. Apparently, the *mother/daughter duo* even attended a local *Community College* together, a few years later;
- **A *Giant*,** who was a few years older than us, who did not use deodorant and was just genuinely mean. *The Giant* would spend her days watching the *Soap Opera's* with *Christine's* mother instead of going to class; and
- A **girl who identified as a vampire**.

Christine's mother also forced her to invite her **second cousin** everywhere because the cousin had no friends. Needless to say, these were not the wild *High School* parties that you saw in teen movies, and I did not really enjoy them, but felt obligated to go when invited.

Over the years, I see *Christine* maybe **every five years** (no need to calculate my age) and we did both attend *Rita's* **first wedding**, along with *Christine's* cousin. After *Christine's* brother was diagnosed with *Schizophrenia*, her family **bought a house and a convenience store** (apparently this was dirt cheap) and moved to *Small Town, Canada*. *Christine* moved with them to help set up the *Store*. *Rita*, *Phil* and I, drove out to visit *Christine* and her family one weekend. They all seemed happy, but the *Store* was being **condemned** because it was falling apart, so there was a **sadness in the air**. However, *Christine*'s father did **manage to lose his teeth** (dreams do come true) but **had not** been able to find **second-hand dentures** that fit him by this point (persistence is key). *Christine* used to come to *the City* to visit her cousin and have the occasional *Karaoke night*, though often with her same strange crew and with no sign of *Rita*.

In recent years, I do not get invited out as much. I was dating a friend of *Christine*'s for a **hot minute** (though, surprisingly not a *vampire* or anything supernatural (to my knowledge and disappointment)) and got **devastatingly dumped**. *Christine* and her friends now invite him out instead of me (what happened to *sisters before misters??*), although, I used to get the occasional (and flattering) last minute invite if **the Ex** could not attend (more to come on that). Lately, however, *Christine* and *Rita* have become close again. *Rita* managed to get *Christine* a job at the office that she works at, and I think that they possibly live together now too (I saw on *Social Media*, that *Christine* and *Phil* went **halfsies** on *Rita*'s birthday gift). I think that after my whole **apartment fiasco** with *Rita* and *Phil*, *Christine* must have picked a side and took (what would have been) *my bedroom*. As a result, I am unfortunately **no longer** part of my first *High School crew* and, most unfortunate of all, I do not think I will ever really know how the ***denture drama*** concludes.

Paulina

During the first month of my *High School* career, I met *Paulina*. *Paulina* was three or four (maybe five) years older than my **9th grade self**, as she had been held back a few times. To me, it seemed that part of the reason why she was repeating *Grade 9* courses was because she really did not show up to class that often (**I was never brave enough to skip classes**).

One weekend, *Rita* attempted to set both *Paulina* and I up with one of her brothers (each), and it became a weird winter five-person group date type thing. "**The Brother**" that was meant to be for me, fell for *Paulina* instead (I am forever grateful for this, *The Brother* later got someone pregnant as a teenager, which could have easily set my life in another **more complicated** direction). *Paulina* gleefully revealed this "*win*" to me by showing off photos they had taken together as a happy couple (I felt that I had to act upset but was deep down not that fussed). Apparently, *Paulina* was not allowed boys in her room alone (in her *Grandma's* tiny apartment), so poor *Rita* had to sit in the room with them **as they did that dance that new couples do**.

Rita and *Paulina* grew very close, with *Paulina* now dating *The Brother*. This caused *Paulina* to constantly hang around "*our crew*", although, I was never particularly fond of *Paulina*. It seemed to me (with **no psychologist degree**, or knowledge, especially at that age) that she was a **pathological liar**, as none of what she said added up. However, *Paulina* really hit a nerve for me when she told *Rita, Christine*, and I, that she was taking us all to an amusement park and to wait for her cousin to pick us up. She left us all waiting all day, as she (and her cousin) simply did not show up without any sort of warning or reason.

Paulina and *The Brother* eventually broke up, for reasons unknown, and *Paulina* dropped out of *High School* shortly thereafter, (or transferred *High Schools*, or took a break, *aged out*?) (It is unclear). *Paulina* claimed that it was because she had given birth to twins, the father being some hot guy that we had never met, though there was never any evidence of this. No one has heard much from *Paulina* since.

A few years after *High School*, based on a *Social Media* search, *Paulina* apparently met **the love of her life** while on vacation, he was a **Waiter** at a *Resort* that she was staying on (I am not sure if this screams "*red flag*" for anyone else…). They got married on the *Resort* (no picture of "*the twins*" at the wedding though…). *Paulina allegedly* then spent months trying to get the *Waiter's* paperwork to come to *Canada*. The *Waiter* later *allegedly* ended up dumping *Paulina*, after he found an *American* girl **who could get it all done quicker**. (Not sure why *America* would be the faster route, but anyway…)

A few years after this, *Paulina* sent me a message, after she saw that one of *Rita's* brothers had passed away, to tell me that she was planning to attend the funeral (since she had spent so much time with *Rita's* family when they were growing up) but **predictably** never showed up (with no heads up once again, *surprise, surprise*) and I have not heard from her since.

I did do a bit of research for the sake of this *entry*, however, **as I am prone to do**, and it turns out that *Paulina* did get remarried (or claims to have in various *social media* posts). It is unclear if this is another *Resort* wedding, or if the "*twins*" were involved at all this time around, but either way, **good for her.**

Catherine's Angels

Longer ago than I am willing to admit [before the days of quarantine, self-isolating, social distancing, restrictions on social gatherings, and facial coverings, if you can remember such a time (I certainly cannot)], I first met *Catherine* in *College*. She was in all my classes from the first semester onwards, but *Catherine's* first real **standout moment** (for me, anyway) was when she thought that somebody **stole her cellphone** and was very adamant that she had friends on the *Police Force* (from when she was in a *Police Foundation College Program* for one semester, prior to our *Program*), who would gladly track her phone for her. Despite having these connections, her phone *allegedly* never turned up again. She was also infamous for dating an older and rougher classmate, although she later claimed that they were "*pretend*" dating to make someone else jealous, but we all saw them consistently *making out* in the hallway before our various classes.

Catherine grew up with money, an only child **with a top lawyer dad and a top surgeon mom**, who lived in a mansion with her parents. She never really had to worry about money and had the benefit of being able to **switch College programs** whenever she **felt bored**. She was quite a few years older than me and was extremely **desperate** for love and marriage. One day, very shortly after

62

we graduated, *Catherine's* dreams came true, and she got engaged.

Apparently, the engagement happened when *Catherine* was on a family vacation. She had **allegedly** met this guy in a chatroom when she was in *High School* [although, I am pretty sure that chatrooms would not have existed in her *High School* days, *but what do I know*? Also, before you all assume that I am also **ancient** (*stop that*), chatrooms **did indeed exist** during my *High School* years.] and they had **apparently** kept in contact via email and had been **talking for years**. Therefore, when *Catherine* went on this trip with her family, she met up with this fellow for the first time while *overseas* and he immediately proposed to *Catherine*, in front of her family as soon as he laid his eyes on her (love at first sight?).

I went to the *Bridal Shower* roughly a month later. *Catherine* showed up over **three hours late** and while I was waiting, I had the pleasure of *Catherine's* relatives spitting on me, every time they walked by me and telling me "*You are next*" [**tradition**? Again, this was pre-COVID and before spitting was considered a *hate crime*, although it was still unpleasant]. Roughly a month later, *Catherine* had her wedding *Overseas*. Even though I could not attend the wedding, *Catherine* had posted photos on *social media*, and it looked lovely, and she made a beautiful bride. *Catherine* moved back to *the City* shortly after the wedding and her *Groom* stayed *Overseas* while they figured out his *Canadian Visa*.

A few months later, *Catherine* and I went out partying. She brought an **"Old Friend"** (another man that she had apparently known for "years") and spent the night telling me that she had "*married the wrong man*" and that she should have married the *Old Friend* instead. *Catherine* went home with the *Old Friend* that night, but I never saw him or heard about him again. *Catherine* then went back *Overseas* for a few months, before moving back to her *the City* mansion for good. When I saw her roughly a year later, she told me that her *Husband* was **cheating on her,** and that the **trunk of her car was full of evidence**. She had also hired a *Private Investigator* and was taking steps towards filing for a *Divorce*. I asked to see the evidence, out of curiosity (since we were already in the car), but she never got around to showing me.

I next saw *Catherine* again maybe a year later and by this point she had been working as an assistant in your standard boring old office job. She told me that she was in love with her *Boss* and that he felt the same way about her. She also informed me that she was a "*dog whisperer*" (a talent I was unaware of, prior to this) and that her *Boss's* dad had even hired her to train his dogs.

Apparently, when she noticed that her *Boss* had become **less friendly** towards her, *Catherine* wrote him a long email (that she let me read, it was cringe), that her *Boss* then read to the entire office during a meeting. The email rambled on about how *Catherine* knew that they were **meant to be** because she had received a message from *God* that showed her this. When *Catherine* was leaving work that evening, to her shock and embarrassment, she witnessed the entire office laughing at her expense, as her *Boss* (oblivious to her presence) read this email out loud in front of everyone and then *Catherine* was later fired (from the dog gig too).

The night that we met up, *Catherine* drove us to a school yard where she knew that her (now former) *Boss* coached *Soccer*, so that *Catherine* could tell him that the email was a **big misunderstanding** (as an attempt to "*save their relationship*"). When *Catherine* spotted the *Boss* in a distance, she pointed him out to me and then informed me that she now had to hide and asked me to keep watching the *Boss* and tell her whether he looked sad. It was at this point that she informed me about the **Restraining Order** that the *Boss* had against her. I kept my distance from *Catherine* after this.

I last saw *Catherine* a few years ago, when I was invited to meet her new "*Boyfriend*". I went to *Catherine's* house first, where I discovered that *Catherine's* mom now calls the *Bridal Shower* (that I had attended) **"Catherine's birthday party"** (but why were they all spitting on me?) and *Catherine's* wedding is now called **"the family reunion"** (is that really all it was?).

We went to a *Patio* that night (apparently, the best *Patio* in the *City*...but doesn't every *Patio* claim this?) and it was a chilled fun night (no stalking). The "*Boyfriend*" was driving, and it made sense (semantics wise) to drop *Catherine* off first. While we were driving to my house alone, the "*Boyfriend*" took the opportunity to ask me for my phone number and then had no idea what I was talking about when I asked whether his *girlfriend*, *Catherine*, would mind. Apparently, and this is according to the "*Boyfriend*", *Catherine* was just a friend of the "*Boyfriend's*" family.

I used to hear from *Catherine* every now and then with updates on this particular "*Boyfriend*", he *apparently* got married shortly after the *Patio* night, although **unfortunately** not to *Catherine* (nor to me).

I have not heard from *Catherine* for a few years now, mostly because my parents **cannot afford the bail money**, should one of her **antics** go awry. *Catherine* was (and likely still is) a fun and genuinely nice person, but she was also **a lot** for me to handle. I see her photo updates on *social media* every now and then and it looks like she has a new **Love Interest** (or possibly a new boss, uncle, family friend, or her dad), who looks much older than her and it looks like *Catherine* now lives *Overseas* (or at least not in *Canada*, as evidenced by the lack of facial coverings in her *social media* photos). Now that I have had the chance to inspect her *social media* more closely for the sake of this entry, **Dear Journal**, it looks like *Catherine* may have even gotten **married** to said *Love Interest* (or attended another **family reunion**) and she looks rather cheerful. Regardless of who he is, *or whatever this current situation is*, I hope that *Catherine* is happy, and that *Love Interest* treats her well. I also hope that *Love Interest* has a lot of patience, understanding, and a dash of good humour, throughout **Catherine's Fantasy World** and the adventures that will *inevitably* follow.

Melanie and Vanessa

Longer ago than I am willing to admit, I worked in an *Amusement Park* as a *Parking Attendant*. I met many interesting characters while working there, especially the customers, or as we called them "*Guests*". I remember **one family in particular** who thought that I overcharged them for parking (they were under the *false impression* that it would be included with their *Season Pass*) and *what felt like a dozen* of them worked together to try and **push my booth over**, with me inside – literally causing the booth to rock back and forth (as I desperately called security for help and **continuously got ignored**). Or the various people who would just drive over the field beside the parking booth if I denied them free parking access (**well, I am not going to chase them**).

My colleagues were nearly just as interesting, and stories will **undoubtedly** follow soon. Notably, there was **one who was convinced** that she was in pageants that simply did not exist, **one who considered a parrot to be her brother** (it took a few "*I fed my brother crackers and he flew away*" stories to realize that he was a bird), the **one who accidentally gave her dog** "*special brownies*" and had to drive a smiling, chilled out pup, to the vet, and **the various inappropriate relationships between coworkers**.

That bunch aside (we will save those stories for another day), I became fast friends with **two sisters** named "*Melanie*" and "*Vanessa*". Both sisters worked at the *Amusement Park*. *Melanie* was my age and *Vanessa* was a year younger. *Melanie* was riddled with anxiety (before it became as widely known) and would do things like swear and run off whenever a *Guest* gave her a hard time (well, do not leave your cash **unattended**). *Vanessa* always had a coolness and calmness about her. By the end of summer, I had bonded with both sisters.

We would hit the old *Night Clubs* pretty well every weekend and take the *TRANSIT* night bus (the "*vomit comet*") home (something that I **would never do** these days). It was always a lot of fun. There was one time that *Vanessa* tried to use a **fake ID** (she was the correct drinking age but did not have a real *ID*) that said that she was from *Quebec*, a "*novelty card*". Unfortunately, her old classmate was coincidentally working at the bar that we had gone to and confirmed that *Vanessa* was indeed **not from** *Quebec*. We got kicked out. Another time, *Melanie* got so upset about losing her phone **or something along those lines** and insisted that we go down to the *Lake* to visit her *Security Guard Boyfriend*, **at 2AM**, so that she could say "*hi*" (my parents were not pleased).

Just before my milestone birthday, *Melanie* and her *Security Guard Boyfriend* **broke up**. We went out that weekend to try and cheer *Melanie* up. Strangely enough though, that night *Melanie* **disappeared**. She re-entered the *Club* (after we had **frantically** searched for her for hours), with pizza in her hand, looking dishevelled with her shirt

buttons all askew. I am not really sure what happened there, but rumour had it, her now *Ex-Security Guard Boyfriend* knew the cousin of the guy, who claimed that she went back to his **nearby apartment**. I will never know if this was true, although *Melanie* claimed that she fell asleep under a table in the *Club*, which feels less likely, given that we thoroughly scoured the *Club* (and where did the pizza come from?).

Then my *milestone birthday* rolled around. I got my hair done, nails done, and tan done (back when everyone was a **shade of orange**). I had a nice new outfit with hot new shoes. I went to the *Club* with *Melanie* and *Vanessa*, as well as a few other friends. *Melanie* was in a really strange mood, something just felt off. When we got inside, before we even had a drink, *Melanie* started freaking out about something or other (possibly another misplaced phone...she really needed to keep her phone at home) and **started screaming and crying**. She even had a **full meltdown**/tantrum while lying on the ground. *Vanessa* asked what was wrong and tried to get her to calm down, and *Melanie* **punched her in the face. They both stormed out.** My other friends felt uncomfortable and followed. **Thank goodness my sibling was there**, because I was left sitting in my *pre-booked booth* alone, absolutely baffled, and **barely** got to show off my outfit (at least I looked good).

The aftermath was that *Melanie* and *Vanessa* felt ***too embarrassed*** to see me again. Which then somehow **spiralled** into me being blamed for *Melanie*'s breakup (I mean, whatever rumours had

70

nothing to do with me) and we just stopped speaking to each other altogether. I saw *Melanie* at a party a few years later and when she heard that I was on route, she had a full-blown anxiety attack and needed to get air. Upon my arrival, everyone had already heard about me and had already formed opinions about how terrible I must be to cause somebody such anxiety. When *Melanie* returned, we just did not speak, and she ended up leaving the party early. It is still unclear why she was so scared of seeing me, after all, **I was not the one punching people in their face.** I have not seen *Melanie* since this very brief encounter.

Lately, however, some of the old *Amusement Park* staff have been discussing a possible reunion (here's me hoping that the parrot comes too). Both *Melanie* and I have been invited for a group dinner on some **future pending date**. If this reunion does happen (and both *Melanie* and I do indeed show up), one has to wonder whether *Melanie* will be more comfortable in my presence, all these years later. **Will this lead to a friendship**? Likely not, but hopefully neither of us will leave the room in tears.

P.S. To the random stranger who came up to me today and felt secure enough with me to share that in the last two months: your dog died, you lost your family, lost your shelter, lost your fiancé, got a kidney infection and yeast infection and now you are on route to go solo camping (**despite the threat of a hailstorm**) – thank you for feeling that

71

comfortable with me and I hope things get better....

Part 3
Leaving The City

I Love NYC

One of my favourite couple friends [at the time], *Rita* and *Phil*, invited me to *New York City* to watch the *ball drop* at midnight at *Times Square*, one *New Years Eve* and I eagerly agreed. My thought was that I had never been to *America* and figured that I would have time [2 months] to find a *plus one*. This was before I realized that they had also invited *Phil*'s work friend, *Steve*, and his wife, *Evelyn*. I tried to back out, thinking it sounded nice as two couples travelling together, but *Rita* talked me into having a "*shared*" experience [as she had never been to *America* either] and **FOMO** (*Fear of Missing Out) is no joke.

We all pitched in and rented a *SUV* together for this road trip, but when *Phil* and *Rita* arrived to pick me up, it became apparent that a **Jeep with a leaky canvas roof**, was all that was available. We had to squish **all five of us** into a *Jeep*, for a 14-hour drive. *A long cold drive, at that.*

Phil refused to cross the *American Border*, at the closer *Border* location because they did not permit him to cross once **ten years earlier**, as he was **smoking a joint** in front of the *Border Guards*, so we had to drive to the other *Border* crossing roughly **two hours out of our way.**

Rita and *Phil* also made homemade "*tobacco vape juice*" for e-cigarettes as a side business, this was before it was *regulated*. *Steve* and *Evelyn*

74

were their **number one** customers, so I was stuck sitting in the back middle seat of this *Jeep*, inhaling various versions of makeshift fruity tobacco smells, **literally every two minutes**, for a **14-hour** road trip.

Anyways, after that horrendous drive, we arrived in *Queens, New York*. *Rita* and Phil booked the *Motel* rooms. Initially it was going to be **five of us in one room**, in order to save some money, however, *Steve* and *Evelyn* insisted on getting their own room in the same *Motel* [fair enough]. We were at the cheapest, *One-Star Rated Motel*, that *Rita* could find, where *Evelyn* happened to find **a dead rat in the drawer of her room**, but the *Pad Thai* restaurant that was across the street from the *Motel* was decent.

The first full day was alright. We had to wake up early to catch the *stale* (but free) complimentary *Motel* breakfast. It was **the day before** *New Years Eve*, so we went on the half hour subway ride to downtown *Manhattan, New York*. The first stop was the *Museum of Natural History*, which was quite amazing and cool [this was *Rita*'s choice, as she wanted to recreate the movie "*Night at the Museum*"]. *Phil* was in an unpleasant mood, which put a damper on the *Museum* [he rushed us through the *Museum*] because, on the way there he was *vaping* **inside** a subway station and nearly punched a guy who asked him to stop. On a positive note, in my experience, the *New Yorkers* were much kinder than expected, quite a few even went out of their way to help us figure out how to pay for the subway.

We then headed to *Central Park*. *Steve* and *Evelyn* wanted to take a taxi there, to feel like **real New Yorkers** [plus *Evelyn* had a sore hip and it was a long walk], but *Rita* and *Phil* said a **hard no** because it was not in their budget [I did not feel like I had much say in this trip as the **fifth wheel**]. I loved *Central Park*, it was my favourite part of the trip for me, it was beautiful, and I recognized more of it from movies than expected. I would definitely go back.

The next day, *New Years Eve*, we survived the next round of a stale complimentary breakfast and then we toured around *downtown Manhattan*, to look at it before the chaos began. We then ended up at *Times Square* after dinner. There had been a **bomb threat** earlier that day [don't worry, they quickly caught the guy], so there was a strict police frisking. Barriers were set up at 6:00 p.m. and it was **$10 USD** per person to get through each barrier [or **$25 USD** for a family of three], which also required a police frisking to check for weapons. They kept adding more barriers further and further away from the *ball*, the closer it got to midnight. *Rita* and *Phil* refused to pay this fee and when it finally got to a point where we were pushed back too far away to see the *ball*, or **hear the music**, *Steve* and *Evelyn* suggested that we go wait at a bar until closer to midnight and then come outside for the countdown. *Rita* and *Phil* refused this too, as it was not in their budget. I also agreed with *Steve* and *Evelyn*, but *Phil* said **no** [but three against two? What happened to democracy?]

76

Eventually, it just got too **silly** and **too cold**. On top of this, the *NYPD* kept coming around to make sure that we were not getting closer to the *ball,* and they also guarded the subway stations to ensure that we were not just waiting in them to stay warm [no loitering]. *Rita* suggested that we go back to the *Motel* room and watch the **ball drop** there. We all eagerly agreed. *Phil* was so upset [he said they do not show the *ball drop* on TV, although I am quite sure that I had watched it every year] he literally ran away, and *Steve* followed to make sure he was safe. The remaining three of us, all took the subway back to *Queens*.

Steve joined us in *Queens* roughly an hour later, after *Phil* was able to successfully run away from him [which was no easy feat considering that *Phil* was overweight and quite a bit older than *Steve*]. *Phil* arrived back **roughly an hour** after that. He missed the midnight countdown and the *ball* had already dropped [that we literally watched on TV, *unless I imagined it*]. Apparently, *Phil* was so upset with us that he took the subway to *Queens* by himself and ended up at some **random guy's house** to smoke a joint, before heading back to the *Motel*.

The next morning was the day that we were supposed to see the *Freedom Tower* before heading home. *Phil* initially said that because of our **collective poor behaviour**, this was not going to happen. This was the one thing that I had really wanted to see. *Rita* eventually convinced *Phil* to allow us to go, and it was well worth it. **It was a very moving site**.

The drive home was fast, literally. *Phil's* theory was that because he was not in *Canada*, he could drive 200KM per hour because no one would be able enforce a speeding ticket, though I am not sure that this is true. We asked him to slow down **several times** throughout the drive. Regardless, we got home safely and in **roughly ten hours**. When paying for gas, we all took turns, which I believe meant that I paid more, being the *singleton* and having to pay **every third time**...but I digress. When *Phil* returned the *Jeep*, he got $100 back as it was not the *SUV* that we had reserved. He did not split this, however, as he felt that he earned it as he did do the majority of the driving.

What Did I Learn in NYC?

1.   The people are genuinely nice and helpful, *Americans* always get the rep of being rude, and *Canadians* nice. In my three days there, I did not find this to be the case.

2.   The coffee sucked. Even in *Starbucks*.

3.   Either go to the countdown at *Times Square* early [before 6:00pm- the people at the very front proudly wore diapers], find a bar nearby, a hotel window to watch it from, or pay the fee. It gets to a point where you literally cannot even hear the concert, so what is the point, really?

4.   When I do go back, I would stay in *downtown Manhattan* and I would **fly in**

from *the City* instead of attempting that long, cold, drive again.

5. **Find fun people**, go with the flow type people, to go with, and loosen that budget just a little bit.

Why I Do Not Camp

Camping was an activity that I did with my family as a child but something **I enjoyed less** as I entered *teenagerhood*. However, this was something that I thought that I **may** enjoy as an adult, with alcohol.

My camping opportunity came around again a few years ago, for the first time in over ten years. I was excited because it was with my *bestie* [at the time], *Rita*, and her boyfriend, *Phil*. *Rita* is from a large family [one of ten children] and would often try and find ways to include her family members in various activities. With camping everything, *payment wise*, was being divided into three, [between *Rita*, *Phil*, and I] despite the **four extra people**, in order to keep the costs lower for *Rita* and *Phil*. [I think that this was the sole purpose of inviting me].

There were seven of us [plus a dog] going on this camping trip, which meant that on top of *Rita* and *Phil's* car, **I needed to rent one too**. This was exciting to me, *as a newly licensed driver*, as it was my first rental. I paid for the rental myself [on top of 1/3 of the two campsites].

I was sleeping over at *Rita* and *Phil's* that night, so that we could organize ourselves before the early morning wake up call. My first stop before arriving at their place [and after picking up the rental car], was to meet *Phil* and pick up some essential camping items [such as water]. I was driving around the parking lot beside their condo but could not find *Phil* anywhere. He was so annoyed that I was taking so long, that he left and **disappeared** without explanation [he went home]. I eventually found him playing video games to "*calm down*". Anyway, I slept over and we were up at the **crack of dawn** the next morning, I could not sleep, and I am naturally **not** a morning person. Despite this, I got up and ready. We first headed to my parents' house to pick up some extra camping equipment, including a 30-year-old tent, that my parents had always used for storage when camping. We then went to *Rita's* family house to pick up her sister, two nephews and her niece ("**the Kids**").

The drive was only an hour long but having separate cars made it more enjoyable. We had the girl's car, which pleasantly included Rita's dog [and not *Phil*]. We eventually arrived at the campsites. *Rita, Phil* and I, were staying on one site and the rest were staying at the campsite next door. We set up the tents and it turned out that because *Rita* and *Phil* had bought themselves cot beds to put into their tent and a giant tent for their family, I got the **privilege** of sleeping in the tiny, 30-year-old, equipment tent, **by myself** [can't I at least have the dog?].

We then went grocery shopping, which I was asked to pay 1/3 of, but was also told "*no*" when I asked about picking up wine [which again, I thought would make camping more bearable] [I mean, I was already paying 1/3 of everything, do I not get a say on what is bought?]. The first night was alright, I had to hear *the Kids* tell the same ghost story around the campfire **about 105 times** [and fake being entertained each time], and then *Phil* sent us all to bed relatively early. I could not really sleep on top of being curled up with the equipment and having no mattress [*Rita's* sister and *the Kids* borrowed my air mattress for their tent], at around midnight it started raining and it **leaked through the bottom of my tent.** [I did try explaining to *Phil*, when we were putting up tents, that I needed a tarp underneath the tent, but he assured me that I was wrong...].

The next day, I had a bit of a **scuffle** with *Phil* because he wanted to teach **the 15-year-old nephew** how to drive in my rental [since it was smaller than his car] and when I said, "*hard pass*", *Phil* thought that this meant that I did not trust his teaching skills. [I mean...*Phil* did not even have his full license himself – and neither of them were covered under the insurance....]. Otherwise, it was a day of swimming in the lake, hiking and another trip to the grocery store [still no wine though]. This was followed by another sleepless night by myself in a leaking tent and **spending an unhealthy number of hours** debating on whether I could make it back from a hotel room before anyone noticed and/or whether I would die from an animal attack in my sleep [neither happened].

The next morning, it was finally time to check out of the campsites and head home. *Phil* had asked *the Kids* to bring their backpacks to the car and when they left it by the back wheel of the car, *Phil* **drove over the backpacks** to teach *the Kids* a lesson in listening skills. I found this quite shocking [coincidentally, *Rita* had asked me to be a **character reference** for she and *Phil* to adopt a child, prior to this trip]. *Phil* also started dragging the dog along the ground to the car, when she was not moving [she's a small dog, that he could have just carried]. The drive home was otherwise uneventful, however, I have barely spoken to *Rita* and *Phil*, since this trip [and being a **character reference** was never brought up again].

I found out that the next summer, *Rita* and *Phil* invited their couple friends to go camping with the family. *Rita* found it shocking when the friends only bought and paid for ***their own*** groceries [including liquor], and only paid for ***their own*** campsite, instead of contributing 1/3 to the family purchases. I do not believe that they have been camping since.

In conclusion, as much as it would be nice to get away during a global pandemic [which has already lasted a year now – crazy] – **camping is just not for me**, you guys can keep your leaky tents.

Part 4
Roommates in The City

Why I DO NOT have Roommates

I first tried the *"sharing a dorm room"* thing in university, thinking that I would have a friend from the start. My roommate had a boyfriend and I realized that I made a **grave mistake** once her boyfriend started sleeping over **4-5 times a week**, in our tiny little room. Therefore, when I was ready to *move out of my parents' house for good*, I knew that I would at least need to have **my own room**.

I always knew that I would end up living downtown, I had *romanticized* it in my head for years. When I was finally ready to *leave the nest*, I discovered this neat little five-bedroom apartment in a neighbourhood situated sort of midtown and sort of downtown (*depending on how big of a* **"downtown snob"** *you are*) that has a lot of trees, something that I really appreciate more the longer that I live downtown. It has sort of a suburban vibe with the convenience of the *City*. The rent was cheap, but I would have **FOUR other roommates** and only **ONE bathroom**, which I always knew would be challenging but I thought that maybe I would learn to compromise (*I did not*). During the initial stages of meeting the others, they all said that they spend a lot of time together and even did some travelling together. It sounded like an opportunity to socialize, and it sounded like fun.

When I first moved in, my roommates were:

- Karen

- Eleonor
- The Boy (I really did not see much of him); and
- Bea (**The Leaseholder**, who also had the biggest room with a bay window and fireplace).

I really liked *Eleonor and Bea* but realized early on that I may have made a **mistake** living with *Karen*.

Karen was the most challenging roommate that I have ever had. She was a few years older than me and had a "Master's Degree in Communication" (*something that she was never shy with reminding me about*) and considered herself an **expert** in same. She was a big believer that every problem could be solved with **coffee and conversation** (*she never once offered me a coffee...*). It seemed that she wanted to be *in charge* of the household but without *any of the responsibility (isn't that what we all want?)*. Of course, she was the only one who **never moved out** in my whole time living there, because that is just how life works sometimes.

The first month was not bad. I made a mistake on my first day living there by "*spoiling a show*" for *Karen*, despite me only being on **episode 2** and her being on **episode 9** (*I did not realize that a comment that I made regarding the name of the show was a spoiler...*) I got pretty *loudly scolded* for that.

A saving grace was that *Bea* worked in the same building as I did, so I had someone to commute with in the mornings, which was nice. By the end of the month, however, *Bea* handed in her **60 days' notice**. She was apparently the last of the original roommates and everyone else had left because they felt that *Karen* took the fun out of living there (*I understood why...*)

The Boy also decided to hand in his *notice* at the same time as *Bea*, so we needed to figure out:

- Who was going to be the *Leaseholder*;
- Who was going to take *over the internet*;
- Posting an ad for the rooms; and
- A chore chart (Karen's idea, obviously...)

(*I was just grateful that Karen did not implement a bathroom schedule*)

It was at this point that I learned that the **new roommate's first month's rent** went towards the **old roommate's last month's rent**, so we really only had **30 days** to collect first and last month's rent, when *notice* is handed in. The logic was that everyone could hand in their *notice* at the same time and then **no one would pay** for the last month's rent.

Being the *Leaseholder* meant that any **unpaid rent** was your sole responsibility.

Eleonor decided that she would organize the **chore chart** and *Karen* said that because I was the only one out of the three of us with a **full-time job**, I would need to **take over the lease**. If I did not take over the lease, **everyone would have to move out**. *Karen* pointed out that I had only just moved in and therefore probably did not want to move out right away.... *she was right*. *Karen* also suggested that if I took over the internet too, then everyone would only have to send me one e-transfer with all payments and save the **extra $1 in bank charges**. I agreed because I did not want to move so soon and wanted to make a good impression, but this is **not something** I would do again.

Karen decided that it would be best that **instead of me** getting the big *Leaseholder* room with the fireplace and bay window, we rent it out for a **higher rent amount** to keep the rent lower for everyone else.

We posted an ad for both rooms and held some interviews. We chose *Emilia* for the big room (*she was the only one who brought donuts*) and *Karen* thought it would be best if we moved her best friend *Manny* into the other vacant room. *Manny* was **delightful** but was obviously *Karen's "ride or die"*.

Emilia was a nice person but was also **very young,** she was partying until 4am with music blasting. She left a mess everywhere. She always had friends over and her friends would even wander into our bedrooms in the middle of the night, looking for a bathroom. She and her friends would have "*tattoo parties*" (*where they gave each other homemade permanent tattoos*). She would wash her hair in the kitchen sink over **everyone's food**. *Emilia, Karen* and *Manny*, all used the **bathtub for laundry** (*to save money*), and all three would leave puddles on the bathroom floor. It was all just a bit too *frat house-ish* for the rest of us *oldies*. In fairness, *Emilia* was always the **first person** to pay me her rent and her internet portion every month and she actually was quite friendly.

Karen **could not stand** living with *Emilia*. She was tired of all the noise, mess and *strangers,* especially the *strangers* wandering into her bedroom in the middle of the night (*same though*). She called a **housemate meeting**, where we decided we should give Emilia **60 days notice** to move out. I was told that I had to give Emilia the bad news, as the *Leaseholder*. It was awful but she moved out with no real issue. She did, however, take all her **passive aggressive anger** out on *me* during those 60 days, as I was the **bearer of bad news**. She would do things like put dead moths in my food, started leaving rotten fruit around the apartment, use my dishes without asking me or washing them (*I ended up having to lock them in my room*) and left paint stains in the room that I was moving into. She also did not pay her portion of the internet for her last month and *Karen* basically said, "*tough luck*", so I had to cover it.

I decided that if I was going to have the stress of being *Leaseholder* then I wanted the **big room** and that I should get it for the rent that I was currently paying (much like *Bea* did). *Karen* did not like this but reluctantly agreed. She was sure to remind me any time money or any other issue came up, that I have that *"**nice big room**"* ....

We held interviews again and this time it was between *Crystal the artist*, or an *Irish Dancer*. I thought the *Dancer* **would be fun** and **liven the place up a bit** but was outvoted and *Crystal* moved in. *Crystal* was fine, except with *Eleonor* barely around (*she spent a lot of time at her boyfriend's place*), I was now the only person who **was not an environmentalist**. This included me being the only one who **flushed the toilet**, or who did not use the bathtub as a washing machine. The others only bought *"green household cleaning products"*, which we all had to chip in towards. They were more expensive than regular cleaning products and I am not convinced that they even cleaned as well as regular products.

When it came to chores, apparently *Eleonor* **randomly pulled names from a hat** every week, although I never witnessed this. Every single week I was on bathroom duty. Whenever I mentioned this, I was told that it was simply *"the luck of the draw"*. I did request to witness this **lucky raffle** but was told that this was something *Eleonor* did at work. It is still unclear why we could not just **rotate names** every week...

Finally, **my last straw**, was when I had a *death in my family*. I was not spending a lot of time there, as I was either at home with my family or at a viewing and funeral. *Karen* organized a meeting to call me out, *in front of **everyone***, for not doing my chores...I had not been there for a whole week prior to this night, *how was I supposed to clean the bathroom (scrub that toilet for the* **60th week in a row***)?*

I decided that this living situation was no longer good for my **mental health** and started **apartment hunting**. *Eleonor* decided to move in with her boyfriend and **handed in her** *notice*. I handed in my *notice* **that same night** (*I decided, if worse came to worse, I could even just move back to my parents' house until I found a place*). Except, **I could not leave**. As the *Leaseholder*, apparently the *Landlord* was going to consider it a **whole new lease** once I left, as he did not have a relationship with anyone else (*makes sense*) and raise everyone's rent by $100 each (*or a $500 total rent increase*). *Karen* blamed me and thought that I "*handed in my notice to the Landlord wrong*" (*is there a right way?*) Nobody could afford the extra $100 per month, and, for whatever reason, I did not want to be the cause of their **inevitable homelessness**, so I agreed to wait for an **extra three months** before handing in my *notice*, to give them time to figure things out.

I was **miserable** for those three months, basically, hung out in my room and avoided all the roommates, especially *Karen*.

I decided that I needed my **own bathroom *with a flushed toilet*** and started *apartment hunting*. I found a really great master bedroom in a *condo*, with only two other roommates (*half the amount that I was used to*), AND (*most importantly*) **my**

own bathroom. Unfortunately, the move in date was one month early and I ended up paying an extra month's rent to help my former roommates out. The saddest part is, they all harassed me for months (*including calling me from different phone numbers*) about $20 I owed towards the Wi-Fi (I *was not even living there to use the Wi-Fi* and *what about my extra months rent???*).

The *Condo* was great. Having my **own bathroom** made a world of difference. My roommates and I all moved in at the same time. We each had our **own lease** with the *Landlord* (*as it should be*). My new roommates' names were *Julie* and *Bailey*, there was **no chore wheel** and **no real power struggle**. The best part was, if you *sort of tilted your head* in certain ways from my bedroom window, and peered carefully between the other buildings, you could even see a **tiny bit of the Lake**.

Julie was bubbly and a lot of fun. *Bailey* was nice but kept more to herself. I did not **put my name** on anything towards the *Condo* this time – *lesson learned*, so *Bailey* was kind enough to set up the Wi-Fi. Unfortunately, she (*somehow*) did not realize that you had to **pay each month** and it was *eventually cut off*. Luckily, the *Condo* had a library with free Wi-Fi.

Julie's personality seemed to change after a few months. She had her cousins sleep over almost every weekend, in the living room, so *Bailey* and I sort of had to tiptoe around them in the morning. She started dating a **much younger guy**, who lived about **four hours away**. Whenever he visited for the weekend, *Julie* would ask *Bailey* and I to **leave for the weekend** *(where were we supposed to go?)*, I just said "no" *(I had my own bathroom, I was paying more in rent, why would I need to leave – there was a hotel right across the street, if she wanted privacy)*.

There was a **garbage chute** on our floor, and it was really close to our unit. I would take my garbage out every day, but one day, when I happened to be on my way out, I discovered that the **other two** were **hoarding garbage** and there were roughly **50 BAGS OF GARBAGE**, filling all of the kitchen cupboards to the brim. It was alarming, but also **not my problem** (after all, I am no *Karen*).

One day, *Julie* **just moved out** without telling anyone, including the *Landlord*. She just **stopped paying rent**, she took *Bailey's* **mink coat** (!!!), and she took my **interview clothes** but otherwise she left the rest of her stuff behind. She still **has not returned my interview clothes**, despite promising to mail them to me whenever I ask (it has **been over three years**).

It was at this point that my lease was coming up for renewal and I decided that I wanted **my own kitchen and my own bathroom,** and it was time to leave.

Coincidentally, a colleague was moving into a *bachelor apartment*, across the street from where we worked. Her rent was going to be **cheaper**

than what I was paying to live with roommates, so I asked for details. After *borderline harassing* the *Landlord* for a few weeks, a bachelor unit finally became available, and it is where I have been living since. There is not much of a view (*certainly no lakeview*), the view is of abandoned mattresses, stained toilets and a dumpster. Now that I am *working from home*, I have noticed that the garbage truck comes about **40 times a day** (*it never collects the mattresses or toilets*) but despite this, **I love it so much more than having roommates**.

At this point, however, I am questioning whether I am **meant to be around people at all**. Having a **shared laundry room is a bit painful**. Some people **hog all the machines** and fold **one item of clothing at a time** in *slow motion*, as you are **waiting to use that machine**. I am not sure why I find the tediousness of this *so annoying*, even when there are *free machines* for me to use, but I am of a strong opinion that **they should just grab and go**. On that note, I think *Ensuite Laundry* is the next goal. **I am simply not meant to share anything with anyone**.

Part 5
Working in The City

Pippa and the Terrible, Horrible, No Good, Very Bad BOSS

"*Ugh Simon....*" was something I found myself muttering more than once a day, while constantly shaking my head and rolling my eyes, at the daily emails that I received at my toxic, grossly underpaid, office job. I know that everyone generally **hates their jobs and/or boss** but this was different. Allow me to explain.

At the time that I was interviewed for this job, I was at a really low point in my life. I felt like I had no friends. I had no money. I had been working a series of different *temp jobs* around the *City* and was tired of the unpredictable nature of *temping*.

I was excited to be interviewed and offered a position for something more permanent. The salary that I was offered [and eagerly accepted] was **less** than what I had made at my last permanent position, despite having more experience, but was told that I would get a **raise after my probation was up** (*I did not*).

My nice office clothes, unfortunately, no longer fit me at this point. In fact, when I started at this job, HR [and her squad – it was quite cliquey at this *Office*] came up to me [wearing yoga pants, as she did everyday] to tell me "*woman to woman*" that the fact that I was wearing black running shoes on days that were not Fridays, **was making**

the other staff uncomfortable (*but the yoga pants was fine....*). I was horrified and embarrassed about this, after all, it was the first (*and only*) time that I had to be spoken to about my office attire.

I was hired to be the assistant to the other staff and to help out wherever I was needed. *Simon* was hired just as my three-month probationary period was coming to an end. Another assistant, *Claudia*, was initially supposed to assist *Simon*, but when she walked into the *Office* on *Simon's* first day, to 300 emails with questions that she had already answered in an *introduction memo* that she had provided to him, I was the lucky one to be paired up with him. I was supposed to **consider it a promotion**, *although, I never got a raise*.

Simon gave me a weird vibe from the start, for no real reason, I just felt really **uncomfortable** around him. He was the type of person, where if you thought the conversation was over and turned your chair around, and then turned back around a few minutes later, he would still be silently standing there. ***It made me jump every time***. I truly believed that he lacked some social skills and/or an inability to read body language.

One day, *Simon* decided that we should learn how to work together better and offered to take me to lunch. I agreed because I was under the impression that *Claudia* was going to join us, but she cancelled at the last minute. As *Simon* and I were walking to the restaurant, he was pointing out all the *Condominiums* in the area that he would like to buy and live in, just making general small talk. We arrived at the restaurant, sat down, ordered our food, and then out of nowhere he said, *"nobody likes you and nobody has your back"*. He told me that the other staff are always going into his office to **complain about me**, which most painfully, included *Claudia* [who I considered to be my friend] and he basically said that I was **on my way to get fired**.

At first, I sort of shrugged the conversation off, I was obviously offended, and it bothered me, but I thought that maybe he was trying to just build his own separate team, **Simon and Pippa v. The Office**, type thing. However, it quickly escalated to the point that he was calling my desk phone at 5:00 **everyday**, as I was packing up to leave for the day, to remind me that everyone hated me *"did this go out? ok good...and everyone still hates you"*. He would say things like *"everyone that I talk to agrees that you are the worst"* or (**my personal favourite**) *"when I got this job, I was promised the best assistant, but I got stuck with you"*.

I was getting **paranoid**. Every time anyone left their desk, especially *Claudia* [who shared a desk with me], I thought *"ugh what did I do wrong this time"* because I assumed that they were going to complain about me. I just wanted to be able to hold onto the job **for one year** so that it would look better on my *Resume* [I can tell you now, *with hindsight being 20/20*, that the verbal abuse **was not worth it**, no matter how flighty a short time period might look on my Resume].

In addition to this daily verbal abuse, I would walk into work each morning and discover my desk and chair buried to the brim in paperwork and filing, thanks to *Simon*. I would have to dig my chair and keyboard out, before I could even begin my day.

My last straw was when *Simon* asked me to stay at work late, *unpaid by the way*, because somebody was coming by to pick a package up and *Simon* was unable to stay. I waited for an hour for this package to be picked up and had, *what I thought*, was a pleasant encounter with the person picking it up. The next day, *Simon* asked me if the package was picked up, I said "yes", and he responded that even that person called the *Office* to say that *Simon* deserved a better assistant. (*What the heck? I stayed late* **FOR FREE**....)

I decided that there was no reason for me hear this every single day, or ever. Even if I was going to be fired, I should not have to hear this (*just fire me*). I was about to quit there and then. I had a *Temp Agency* on the phone, explaining that I was miserable and begging them to find me any temporary job ASAP. I also called *Claudia* to tell her that I was going to quit. *Claudia* said that none of what *Simon* was saying was true and to just hold on a little longer because the other assistants were trying to get him fired. Apparently, everyone **hated him and not me**. I agreed to wait it out but did not realize at the time, that I was committing to **seven more months** of *Simon*.

For the sake of my *mental health*, I decided that I did not want to take phone calls from *Simon* anymore, I wanted everything that he said to be in writing. It even sort of inspired the beginning of my most successful weight loss journey, so that I would always have an excuse to not go to lunch with him. **I got better at asking the other staff questions** because I just wanted to ensure that I was doing everything that was expected from me, as an assistant [cover my bases]. I got really good at keeping a paper trail of everything and I got better at dressing more professionally, dressing the part. I became great at scheduling and sending out monthly lists of upcoming events and deadlines for the entire *Office*. I was also never late to work. Being miserable forced me to become **better at my job**.

Every single thing that *Simon* did wrong was guaranteed to be my fault. He would literally call everyone but me in the *Office*, while he was away from the *Office*, to blame me for whatever mishap happened.

One example was he took a bus to *Small Town, Canada*, for a meeting [roughly an hour away from the *Office*, by car, on a good day] but when he arrived, he could not find the location of the meeting. He then took a **taxi back to the *Office* and rented a car** to drive back to *Small Town*, and arrived at this meeting **two hours late**. He asked the *Office* to reimburse him for the **over $700 in transportation costs** for this journey. He managed to blame me, but **I never would have** suggested any of this. Another example is, sometimes lights would just turn off automatically in the boardroom if there was not a lot of movement. If *Simon* happened to be in the middle of a meeting when this occurred, instead of turning the lights back on, he would just sit in the dark. The attendees of these meetings would often complain, as this made them **feel uncomfortable** and he would blame me [should I be running to the boardroom when I did not even know the lights were off?].

When he received a bookshelf for his office, I was asked, and took the liberty of, organizing everything onto the shelves, while he was away for the day (*obviously*). [Note that I did not just bury his desk and chair, despite the temptation.] He told everyone but me [the only person doing this task] that it looked really great. Not one thank you.

He would never tell me if I did anything right and he never stopped reminding me of how **terrible and hated I was.**

Simon would wear the same dress shirt and pants almost every day. One day he arrived to work with a wet stain on his shirt, and the other staff asked him what happened, thinking he spilled coffee or something, and he said that he "*popped a boil on his shoulder and it exploded*" he wore the same stained shirt for the **next two days** and everyone noticed.

After, roughly **nine months** of working for *Simon*, when my *Diet* was finally paying off for me and everyone started noticing that I lost weight, *Simon* must have overheard a conversation and started asking to join the gym with me. He wanted to use this time to talk about work, while pumping weights. He also wanted help and tips to *"lose his gut"* [grabbing onto his stomach while explaining this...]. I did not want this at all. He was the whole reason that I needed the gym, I needed an escape. It was my alone time and my way of releasing the many frustrations of the day before heading home. He started ending all of his emails to me or conversations with me by reminding me that he wanted to join my gym and requesting for my help to get him the gym ***"poverty discount"*** (*bro, you make **quadrupole** what I make and I do not get this discount*) and I started forwarding the emails to HR. **Nine months later** and I was finally ready, if it boiled down to a decision that one of us had to go, and they kept him, I knew that **I would be okay**.

During a business meeting at around this same time, he also suggested that myself and the other female person attending this meeting [who did not work at our *Office* (not that that matters)] all head back to his place for some wine and a quick *ménage à trois*. That person complained directly to the owner of the business, the suggestion apparently made her uncomfortable (*same*).

Simon was fired on **April 1st**. When they told me, I initially thought that it was a cruel *April Fool's* joke (*good one guys*). However, It was no joke. I was warned that if I ever saw *Simon*, especially near train tracks, to walk the other way. I guess that meant he blamed me for getting fired and said something threatening (*no surprise here*). He ended up starting his own business with a very similar name and the exact same logo, literally right across the street from the *Office*. To this day, I still change directions if I happen to see him in a distance.

Years later and whenever I find myself job hunting, there is almost always a post looking for an assistant at his business and according to the job reviews, **no one seems to survive there longer than three months**. However, suspiciously, his business has almost a **5-Star Rating**.

I was asked by HR and the owner of the business, why it took me so long to speak up. If I had spoken up sooner, then maybe the *Office* could have avoided some embarrassment. Truthfully, I was scared. I did not want to lose my job. I did not want everyone to believe him (*that I was the worst*) over me (*he was*). To me, assistants were a *dime a dozen*, and I would be replaced immediately with no real issue. At this point however, I cannot see ever waiting so long to speak up again. It took me a long time to get over my ***paranoia and self esteem issues*** and no job is worth one's *mental health*. There are always other alternatives.

Workin' 9 to 5 (...and unpaid overtime)

My very first office job after completing *College* was as a *receptionist/assistant*. It was a nice office, considering their patience with someone **so green** though, **in retrospect**, the other women were quite catty. The person who I mainly assisted, *Joanne,* was a delight and also a new graduate (everyone else was at least twenty years older than me). When *Joanne* left the office for a new opportunity, the *office manager* decided that it was not busy enough to justify hiring a replacement for *Joanne* and offered to keep me as a fulltime *receptionist*.

I was at a point in my life where I could not imagine staying in that same position for the **next forty odd years** and I reached out to an old *professor*, who acted as my mentor. Coincidentally, the *professor* did know of another office who was looking to hire a *"productions assistant"*, I did not know what this was, but I thought it sounded cool (like a movie star) and I applied.

The *Office* was located in the heart of the *City*, which is where I really wanted to work (I wanted to rock the power suits and white running shoes). It was a new company; it was originally a partnership between *Lilly* and *Greg,* but they had some sort of falling out. As a result, the partnership dissolved and half the staff left with *Greg* (two floors higher up in the same building), including *Lisa*, who they were looking to replace. Apparently, after everything was moved to *Greg*'s new office, *Lilly*'s team all went to lunch to celebrate being the survivors, including *Lisa*. *Lisa* then **switched teams** after lunch (savage). *Michelle*, who interviewed me, wanted me to start immediately, as *Lisa* had left a backlog of work behind, but I said I needed to give my current position two weeks' notice. Despite really not wanting to wait for *Lisa's* replacement to start, *Michelle* offered me the job.

Two weeks later, I eagerly started my first day at the new job. It turned out that a *productions assistant* is somebody who is in charge of the photocopying and scanning for the entire *Office*, as they were trying to go paperless. I started with over a month's worth of backlog (**read:** 10-year-old stale documents that they wanted scanned into the system) and *Michelle* wanted me to clear this as soon as possible. On top of this, *Michelle* wanted me to be **three days ahead** of my current deadlines. I also had to cover the reception desk for an hour during the *receptionist's* lunch break, and I was advised that I should not be taking lunch with the other assistants anyway, because sometimes people simply need the "*time to vent*" (this has stuck with me throughout every job that I have worked at since then). I *embarrassingly* fainted on my first day during photocopier training and this probably should have been a sign of a challenging job. Despite all of this, I was determined to stick with it as I was **promised a promotion** if I survived the three months' probation.

Everyday, *Michelle* would ask me where I was at with my deadlines and backlog and remind me that I needed to be ***three days ahead*** of the current deadlines. I also had constant *rush jobs*. I was at a point where I was working from **8am-10pm with no lunch break** as I did not have time to cover reception and take a lunch break and I was not allowed to eat at my desk. I **was only getting paid from 9-5**, and not that great a salary at that. My hands would literally be shaking on the train every morning and normally I am quite good with stress. On top of this, I also got the pleasure of constantly hearing about how *Lisa* used to do things and how she was much more organized than me (where is she though?) (I used to see *Greg's* team on the elevator on their way to go party – I was tempted to switch teams myself). I looked forward to Thursdays as I had a chance to breathe a little bit because it was the one day a week that *Michelle* was not in the *Office*.

A few weeks later, on *Halloween*, I had a rush photocopying job of **ten huge binders**. It was assigned to me at around noon and needed to be done by the end of the day, in order to be sent out the following day by courier. Somehow along the way I missed a tab or something, and it *threw* everything else off, I did not realize this until later in the afternoon. When I told the assistant, *Kelly*, who assigned the job to me, what had happened, she rolled a chair into the photocopy room, sat there with her arms crossed behind me, and supervised me to ensure that I stayed in the *Office* until I fixed the binders and completed the job. I stayed until well **after midnight** (no lunch or dinner break by this point (*Kelly* had a dinner break) and, most annoyingly, no overtime payment). On top of this, I **had to cancel my *Halloween* plans**. When the binders were finally figured out, *Kelly* said that I needed to stay and finish creating the mailing labels and courier envelopes and that it was time for her leave. I asked if I could leave too and finish the rest in the morning and *Kelly* chuckled and said to stay until the job was done. I was so **frustrated** by all of this and wanted to quit the job (that promotion though). My parents, *who kindly picked me up with food*, told me to **never skip** my lunch break, it makes a world of difference to have an hour break to myself and no job is worth working through it. **Words that I have lived by ever since.**

After this, I started taking my lunch break, eating lunch and going for an hour walk, after my reception shift and it really did help my *mental health*. Michelle, **inevitably**, came up to me a few weeks later to ask how far ahead of my deadlines I was. I said that the backlog was finally cleared and that I was now **two days ahead** of current deadlines. She said that she expected me to be **three days ahead** and handed me my **severance cheque** and told me to pack up my stuff. As I was waiting for the elevator with my box of belongings, I could see the *receptionist* through the window making a sad face and waving. I felt mocked but it was an image that I will never forget.

I was devastated, *fired for the very first time in my life*, just before the **holiday season**. I had given up a permanent position for this job and they knew it. With hindsight, however, I am not sure I could have handled the stress much longer, especially if I did not receive the ***promised promotion***.

I have worked in a few offices since this, who have had people working in a similar position or department as I was (*production assistant*). I always try to be extra nice to the people in those positions because **I have been there**. However, I have found that they are often amazing at the job, incredibly fast and on top of the deadlines (though, I am not sure that I have ever experienced anyone **three days** ahead of deadlines, especially with scanning backlogged old documents). It often makes me question why I could not handle this position but, *truthfully*, I think *Michelle* wanted a *Lisa* and I am simply a *Pippa*.

Diaries of a Teenage Ranger

I was part of a *Ranger Program* the summer that I turned 17. It was an opportunity for a fulltime summer job that you can partake in only during the summer of the year that you turn 17 and only if you live in *Canada* (the supervisors were older but had completed the *Program* in previous summers). The idea was that you would get shipped away for the summer to one of the *Parks*, picked at random, and then spend the summer appreciating the outdoors, participate in tons of canoeing (and learn how to canoe), as well as doing odd jobs (such as painting or picking up trash) for the town closest to where you were staying. It also gave you the chance to meet people your own age from across the *Country*.

I was sent to a small town which had a time difference of being an **hour behind** *City*. That summer, the *Rangers*' biggest mission was adding campsites to *GPS* (which I realize makes me sound ancient, considering how common *GPS* is nowadays). On a side note, and something that I hope makes me sound a **little younger** than the previous sentence did, I had also read someone's online *Blog* (yes, I did have internet), about why one should attend the *Rangers Program* and what her experience was like, before I had attended. I found her *Blog Post* to be quite interesting, and was partly the inspiration for this idea, even though, **unfortunately**, the *Program* no longer exists.

Anyways, I had recently spent a weekend eagerly searching for my *Ranger* journal that I had written in daily, for the sake of documenting that summer of long ago. The original plan for this entry was to copy type the daily entries, as a two-part series, *July* being part one and *August* being part two. I thought that I would be able to share some drama, especially considering that I was convinced that my **Roommate** was going to murder me, after she had shared a story of **rubbing her sister's underwear against Poison Ivy** whenever they were fighting but was otherwise silent around me. There was also one **annoying girl** from *Small Town, Canada,* who seemed to hate anyone from the *City* (what?) and constantly gave me a hard time about being from the *City* (she would even say things like "you cannot wear name tags in *City* because then the *stalkers* would know your name", can *stalkers* not read in *Small Town*??). We had also watched a Bear Training Video, which shaped the rest of my life ("*Whoa Bear*").

Unfortunately, after finding said *journal*, it turned out to be **the most boring thing** that I have ever read in my **entire life** (I felt like I was reliving the day-by-day **without the drama**), so let's see if I can find some interesting journal entries. (I will try and add some **retrospective sass**).

July 7 – Day 3

Today we learned about the *Sauna, Laundry Room, Tool Shed* and the *Vans*. **Curfew is at 10:00 PM** but we all chilled in *Amber*'s (the *Fashionista,* who could sew clothes out of any fabric, much like *Maria* from *The Sound of Music*) room, until a fire alarm went off (set off by the *supervisors* – I saw one of them standing on a chair under the fire alarm) and **we were all caught running out of one room!**

(As punishment, curfew was changed to **9:00 PM** for one week (my **birthday**, *of course*, fell during this week), making it difficult to walk the 2 KMs to the payphones (one way) (for my **Gen. Z's** reading this, *a payphone is a public telephone that is operated by coins or a prepaid card*) after dinner and then back to *Camp* in time to make curfew (we were not allowed to bring our cell phones to the *Program*). This punishment was especially difficult considering that one girl insisted on hogging **the only payphone** in the vicinity, despite the lineup growing behind her, to speak to (and have full on conversations with) all of her *Grandfather's* dogs – *couldn't she have just gone on speaker phone, and speak to them all at once?*)

July 19 – Day 15

Last night, *Maureen* (the *Fun One*, who knew all the camp games and songs and rocked a *mullet*) thought that her **bed was shaking** so she ran into *Amber* and *Tania's* (my *Ranger Bestie*) room, and she was so freaked out that **she was crying**. This whole **ghost** in our cabin thing is really starting to get creepy because now there has been (*unexplained*) rocks thrown into the *Lake*, doors

111

opening and closing, footsteps, and (one night) **I saw a figure in the doorway** (**Roommate**, *carrying my underwear to the Poison Ivy patch, perhaps?*). *Maureen* and *Martha* (the *Annoying One*, who hated folks from the *City*) named him *Gab* and *Martha* made a welcome sign for Gab (seemed a little unnecessary). (Although, I am now half convinced that I am still haunted by a ghost to this day, so perhaps I should have been more welcoming – *what's up, Gab?*).

July 23 – Day 19

Today was **Day 2** of a *5-day Canoe Trip*. We woke up at...I do not know when, because we are not allowed to have watches (or any timekeeping devices – they did not want you to know how long we had been paddling for. The theory was – this would make our arms feel less tired). Anyways, we did a lot of paddling and two portages, and we started the *GPS* process and cleaned campsites. I steered the canoe today after the first portage, I finally got the hang of the *J-Stroke*. It was really muddy on the second portage (waist deep mud – one girl even got *Trench Foot* because of the mud (did you know that still existed?)). If my writing is really messy (which it was), it is because I am writing in the tent in the dark.

Canoeing Partner was *Rona* (the Buzz Kill supervisor – I really did not like her – she made a fuss when I did not know how to act a movie out, when playing *Charades* (I had never watched said movie) and I thought that *Charades* was meant to be fun...)

Tent Buddies are *Tania* and *Katherine* (the Lovely Chatty One, the challenge with *Katherine* was if you shared a tent with her, she had this habit of insisting that you stay up and watch the **100 canoe videos** that she inevitably took that day, which was mostly of the water...I mean, *I had literally just lived it...*)

July 29 – Day 25

Today was our **three-and-a-half-hour drive day**. We got up at the usual time, except I was *Cookie* (meaning that I had to help *Nina*, the *Cook*, in the kitchen – there were two of us everyday, helping out with the meals and the dishes of the day, on a rotating basis. The annoying part was, the *Cookie* had to get up before the "bell" – although, one of the *Cookies* got to ring it, to wake everyone up – and it was similar to a *gong*, so that was fun) and had to get up extra early *argh*. After that, we packed lunches and went into the van.

I started out sitting beside *Gretta* (*the Long Haired One*, who was also from the *City*, but was eagerly moving to *Small Town*, after this trip. She also had super long hair and used to shed like crazy, everywhere, you would constantly see balls of *Gretta's* hair roll by, like *Tumbleweed* from the *Old West*) and then I moved to sit between *Amber* and *Mary* (*the lovely Childlike One* who loved *Winnie the Pooh* and was forced to join *Rangers* by her parents, but who was also quite humorous). After, we went to a clear-cutting site (to chop tree branches, in order to make bear trails – never understood why bears needed clear trails, but what do I know?). After that, we went to the **Guys' Camp** and stayed in their *Park* for the night, it was fun! (No funny business though).

Tania and I got matching boardshorts (my pair is still around, somewhere).

July 31 – Day 27

Today we had the day off and we got to **sleep in until 10:30** and then we had to get up for *Brunch* (by the way – I have never been a morning person, so it surprised me to read that 10:30 was a sleep in, it certainly is not these days...). We had *Evaluations* today, so first they called people going on a *Canoe Trip* and I was called soon in after that. It was *Megan* (the *Funny One*), *Kathleen* (the *Top Supervisor*) and *Rona* (the *Buzz Kill*). *Rona* read the *Evaluation* (and likely wrote it, *in retrospect*). It was kind of sad because I apparently have **no leadership qualities** or **initiative skills** (I mean, I was a **shy kid** from the *City*, who had not done any camping activities in years). Oh well, I still have another month to improve (and I did improve, in fact, I was the *Most Improved Ranger*). After that we went to the beach and then we came back for dinner. We had pierogis, bacon bits, sausage coins and mashed potatoes. After dinner, we were going to have a *Sauna* but because all of the people who wanted one were on the *Canoe Trip*, we did not have one. I felt kind of bad for *Amber* though (I guess she was the one craving a *Sauna*), so instead of a *Sauna*, we painted our names on the table (just as fun), so all in all, today was a good day!

Diaries of a Teenage Ranger (Part 2)

During the second half of the *Ranger Program*, I think I tried much harder to be positive, in order to try and get a better *Performance Review*. I, therefore, hope that I can make it at least a little interesting, **but really**, how could I compete with **Gab the Ghost**?

August 2 – Day 29

Today I was on *Cookie Duty*, so I had to be in the kitchen by **6:30AM**. *Nina* has already left for her weekly time off [if I remember correctly...I think *Nina* got the weekends off and stayed in a cabin just outside of *Camp*], so *Kathleen* was the supervisor who was in charge of breakfast. We had porridge and fruit for breakfast [prison food?]. After breakfast, we packed a lunch and the *Cookies* (*Lina* and me) had to do dishes [literally washing dishes for 25 people by hand...*pre-COVID*] ...

After doing the dishes, we went into *Town* to go and paint/stain the outside of the "*Biological Building*" but then in the midst of painting, this **old fellow** came running over to inform us that we were in fact **painting the wrong building** [story of my life]. After we finished painting the *Biological Building*, we had to go paint what the *Town* calls the "*Round Building*" [the correct building]. It turned out that we did not have enough paint to finish the job [after all, we had just finished painting one building], so we went back to *Camp* and gathered sticks for firewood.

116

Currently, *Katherine* is teaching *Tania* how to play the guitar. I also want to learn to play the guitar, since I want to purchase one when I get home [never happened] but I think that I need *one-on-one* lessons in order to learn (*I'm special*). [I was also told several times during *Rangers* that **left-handed people** need a special left-handed guitar and therefore I would not be able to learn on a standard *acoustic*...but I think that they just did not have the patience to teach me]. [**Fun Fact:** *Tania* actually met her now husband/baby daddy, *Rupert*, through taking guitar lessons with him, roughly two weeks before the *Program* started...].

August 4 – Day 31

Today we went to create *"bear trail paths"* [by clearing a path through a heavily wooded forest, using chainsaws, clippers, and other sharp objects. Much like the start to every horror movie]. We need to create **50** trails altogether and we cleared **32** trails today. Apparently, the people that we are making these paths for, will then leave sardine cans throughout the trails in order to collect the bears' DNA, so that they can keep track of them, [I found this quite interesting]. We cleared the paths and marked the trees with orange plastic ties.

August 12 – Day 39

Today was **day 4 of a 5-day** canoe trip. It was quite the ordeal! First of all, it took us **three hours** to get off the campsite and that was **two hours longer** than it was supposed to take (*not cool*) [I think it must have been a struggle for us all to get moving. Either that or the site was especially filthy (the state that the campsites were often left in by campers, still makes me sick. It's a wonder that there was not more bear attacks)].

Anyways, we finally left the campsite and started canoeing. My canoe partner was *Alexis* [a junior supervisor, or "*Assistant Sub Supervisor*" (ASS)]. We did **three portages** and at the end of the third portage we had lunch. After lunch, we started paddling again and the waves were huge, and the wind was against us. It was like [how I imagine] **white water rafting**, the waves were going over our canoe. We finally got to our campsite and we (as in *Maureen, Gretta* and I), pumped water **from a literal Well** for everyone until dinner. For dinner we had *Burritos*. [This canoe trip was an international cuisine theme, which was a huge step up from the prison porridge].

August 16 – Day 43

Today we woke up painfully early, **6:30 AM** to be exact, which is the regular time [but I think this particular entry must have been written on a weekend]. Anyways, we had sausages and eggs for breakfast, it was quite good except I think I am getting sick of eggs [in fact, I haven't really enjoyed **scrambled eggs** since the *Ranger's* experience]. Anyways, so today's job was to work at the *Tourist Centre*, which is a 10–15-minute drive down the *Highway* from *Camp*. What we had to do was clear trees and bushes in the forest, in order to create a cross country path [using chainsaws, clippers, and other sharp objects, once more] [if you have ever wondered how these trails are formed, the answer is **teenagers**]. *The Centre* provided us with lunch, which consisted of chicken and fries, quite *scrumptious* indeed. We finished early and apparently did an impressive job, so we got to finish work for the day half an hour early (*boo yah*).

<u>August 19 – Day 46</u>

Even though we went to bed late yesterday, we had to wake up early today. We woke up to the "*Birdy Song*", which is not a fun song to wake up to [I can't remember how it went, something with whistling, screaming and supervisors somersaulting into your tent or room...]. We ate breakfast and then headed off to *Jambo* [an end of summer friendly tournament, between all the *Camps* in the area] and started our activities for the day.

[I then went into great detail of the games that we would be playing in my journal, but I will not bore you all here. Basically, all the *Camps* in the area merged and became one giant *Camp* for a long weekend, as an end of summer party. Upon arrival, we were divided into teams, two people per camp per team, picked at random. It was your typical ice breaker summer camp games, i.e. passing a jug full of water backwards to the person behind you while lifting it above your head, type thing.] [I hate *icebreaker games*].

119

August 20 – Day 49

Today was **day three** of *Jambo*. We were up in time for brunch and ate it at the *Guys' Camp*. After brunch, it was *Camp v. Camp* activities and I was on the *"First Aid Team"*, along with *Darla*, *Gretta* and *Maureen*. We came in **second place**. *Tania's* little *T-Rescue Team* [Read: Canoe Rescue] [It seems that *Tania* and I had this harmless banter between us, being on opposing teams and all] came in **first place** (must have been the pity points, kidding) and our *Fire Tent Team* most likely came in **last place**. It was sad, but they did an awesome job considering that our *Camp* never learned how to put up a *Fire Tent*. After the *Camp v. Camp* activities, they gave out awards and our team tied in **second place** and the *Guys' Camp* came in **first place** [typical].

August 28 – Day 55

Today we got up, ate breakfast, signed various memorials [including, signing each other's hardhats (we got to keep those), and wrote *"survival tips"* in the dresser drawers for the future *Rangers*]. We then packed the vans and were dropped off at the *Airport* [the supervisors had to stay an extra week to clean, that's why they got paid the **big bucks**]. We spent the day at the *Airport* and then eventually got onto the plane. I was so excited to go home and see my family again [especially, my 4-month-old kittens] but so sad to leave my friends. (By the way, *Tania* and I sat beside each other on the plane). It was especially sad to leave *Tania*, since she was my

Best Ranger Friend. [We managed to keep in touch over the years, I even attended her wedding]. The *Ranger* experience has come to an end. [I had lost my voice for, what felt like months, after arriving home].

I was often asked after I got home, by various friends and family members, whether I would ever consider going back to *Rangers* as a supervisor [before the program was unfortunately cancelled], but I have always maintained that, *for me*, this was better as a *once in a lifetime* experience. Although, the *Program* did do wonders for my self-esteem, confidence, and taught me to be a little less shy, I am not sure that I could handle living in five-day old, muddy socks again. Nor, do I feel any great desire to ever play *Charades* again. It is just not the life for me.

Why I Do Not Mix WORK and Family

My first office job was kindly offered by a friend of my parents', named *Rhonda*, while I was still in school. Her role in the company was some sort of corporate hotshot *CEO* and she had an *Executive Assistant* named *Tony*. I was hired to assist *Tony* for the summer in filing and organizing **10-year-old documents** around the office, in order to prepare for an audit happening later that year. Also, to assist with a mass letter mailing task for a company wide meeting.

The job was located in *Small Town, Canada* and my hours were **8:00am-5:00pm** because *Rhonda* wanted me to be paid the full **8 hours** (she was a nice lady). The commute, however, was brutal, I had to catch a **6am bus** to make it on time, as the buses to this part of *Small Town* were very infrequent.

My first day was a bit awkward. Nobody had arrived to the office yet (I was the first one in almost every morning), the lights had not been turned on yet and it was dark, and I was unsure of where to go. I sent *Rhonda* an email from the lobby to let her know that I had arrived, and she took this as a sign of a **lack of confidence** because I did not just holler **"hello"** down the hallway. To this day, I think I would still have taken that same approach... Regardless, *Rhonda* showed me the ropes, took me for breakfast and lunch, and introduced me to *Tony* when he arrived.

Tony was **friendly**, **flamboyant**, **overweight** and an **extremely religious** man, who was also a **choir director** for his *Church*. To my surprise, he had a wife and four kids. He rocked that frosted tip, spiky hair look (long after the *90's boyband craze* – stop aging me). He was nice enough and frequently gave me advice on a good *clubbing* look and a nice pair of heels (he became my **fashion guru** for the summer). He began most Mondays with a broken-down car story from the weekend, where he could just call anyone up from his *Church* to come help him (why did his car breakdown so often though?), that community helpfulness and those stories *almost*, and I said **almost,** made me consider joining his *Small Town, Church*.

My biggest responsibility for *Tony* was constant 15-minute walks *one way*, to fetch his lunch or coffee, and labeling file folders.

Now, you are probably thinking that this job sounds **cushy,** and you are wondering about the title of this *entry*. Let me tell you.

When I got my first pay cheque, I decided to go all out on my first major hair appointment, got it cut, highlighted and a professional blowout. I arrived to work on the Monday and *Rhonda* said that my hair looked like a **"*bad mullet*"**, (are there good mullets?). *Rhonda* then called the *HR lady* into her office, to get the *HR lady's* opinion (they were best friends), and even started threatening to cut it with a pair of scissors in her hand, as she stood behind me. I was **so embarrassed** and taken aback.

Rhonda then called her hairdresser to arrange an appointment for me because she thought that my long hair was like a "*security blanket*" and that I needed to cut it **above my ears, like she had**, in order to let it go. (Trust me, this would not suit me). Finally, after I spent a lot of time convincing *Rhonda* that I liked my hair, she let it go.

Most days after work, *Rhonda* insisted on giving me a ride to a stop near her house, which is slightly closer to mine. I really did not mind just catching the bus, but she would not take "*no*" as an answer. One day, during our ride, *Rhonda* asked me why I was eating salad for lunch and when I said I wanted to lose a bit of weight, she said that I needed to lose "***about 10 pounds***", she was not wrong, but it also was not her place. Another time, *Rhonda* told me that I was going to "***float from job to job with no real purpose***", when I said I was not sure what my five-year career plan was. I think of this every time I find myself bored and on another job hunt. I also had to awkwardly overhear conversations between *Rhonda* and her 18 year old daughter and 20 year old son, where she would encourage them to lay flat on the floor, so that "*bad guys*" could not see them through the house windows (she lived in a literal mansion by the way, not some rough neighbourhood), because "*the kids*" were **home alone for 10 minutes** and scared.

Rhonda also insisted on setting up a carpool for me to take me into the *City* on the days that she could not. On one such ride, I knew that my colleague who was driving me, spoke fluent *French* and I had a *French* letter to send out. I was curious (and partly trying to break the ice) whether this was something that my colleague would translate, or if we sent it out somewhere for interpretation. After dropping me off at the bus stop, my colleague emailed *Tony* my question. The next day I walked into the office to a **livid** *Tony*, demanding that I sign a *Confidentiality Agreement*. I did not understand his reaction at the time, nor do I now. *Tony* furiously reminded me **to never discuss work** outside of the office. I mean, I was asking a coworker about a *French* translation, in a car (what else do you really have in common with colleagues?) ...but anyway.

I stopped taking any rides after this and just walked to the bus stop.

After my summer office experience had concluded, I heard a rumour that *Tony* accused me of **hiding documents**, and that he had to really search to find them. I am not sure how this was possible given that my main job was fetching his coffee and labeling folders. He also said that because of his *Religion*, he would have to be "*very honest,*" when I asked for a job reference. Needless to say, I decided to not use him, nor have I heard from *Tony* since. Whenever my parents hear from *Rhonda*, she apparently always mentions that *Tony* consistently asks about me. **I bet he does.**

My parents kept in touch with *Rhonda*, despite my adamant desire that we all just cut her. She offered to tutor me on a course a few years later, which I hesitantly accepted but when I actually spoke to *Rhonda*, she said to join an $8,000 tutorial program instead (thanks anyway…). Unfortunately, shortly after I left, *Rhonda* was let go from the company for spreading some **risky rumours** about one of the *higher ups*. *Rhonda* said that they just did not understand her "*whacky humour*" (neither did I). *Rhonda* has since found great success elsewhere and *Tony* stayed with the company.

Looking back, and having some **horrendous** jobs and bosses since this, that summer really was not so bad. I learned to keep track of coffee orders, was paid a **full eight hours** (which I have not been since) and learned how to label folders. If I were asked to go back (as a boss, not a lowly coffee grabber) sure, I would. I would just have to chop off my hair first, lose a bit of weight and have the names of *French* interpreters ready to go. **If I ever did have this opportunity, I would indeed insist on having *Tony* fetch my coffees.**

The Retail Saga Part 1

The **saga** begins at the end of *October*, the shop that I currently work at normally hires *seasonal staff* in bulk for the *Holiday Season*, but I slid in just before the influx. The store that I was placed in is huge, and I quickly realised that I **would never find my way around**, being someone who **lacks any sense of direction**. I was given the standard tour *"products here and bathrooms there"* type thing, and sort of shadowed someone on cash for a little while, before **being in charge of her till** on my own. I found it all **a bit overwhelming**, especially considering that there were a lot of bulk orders that day, and I had to figure out how to bag and box quickly. On top of this, I had the added pressure of trying to make **someone else's till balance**.

I then had a long break (a month) before being scheduled again. In the meantime, I got called in to work at a different store location and **it was great**. A much smaller and slightly sketchier store, but the shoppers seemed less *stuck up* and there was more of a sense of **camaraderie** among the staff. This is what I was looking for all along, however, I was **never** called back there again (guess I did not "wow" them).

By the end of *November*, the shifts for the regular store started rolling in like crazy. Due to the fact that I had **started before** the *seasonal staff*, the *permanent staff* assumed that I knew more than I actually did, having only worked **one shift there**

127

and a **second shift** elsewhere. In fact, one got particularly *snippy* when I asked how to find a box containing one product, the back of the store where products are kept **is a maze**, and she assumed that I knew my way around. **She did later apologize**. That same day, the trainer who let me use her *till*, seemed particularly upset that I locked mine (trust no one) and **hollered my name across the store** to "*help a customer*" (so embarrassing).

I also walked into other staff talking about me, about how "*this is why you do not hire someone with a full-time job, they do not care about the part time job as much*". I mean **fair**, but also uncomfortable to walk into.

I started to think that maybe I made a mistake sacrificing all my weekends for what I thought would be a bit of fun and pocket money. I was also having a really hard time coordinating the *mandatory Friday shifts* because I had other commitments. It boiled down to me being given a choice to **either work Fridays or resign**, **so I resigned**. However, with the *Holiday Season* upon us, I told them that if they wanted me to, I would continue to work because I did not want them to be *short staffed* and, *of course*, as a result, they have scheduled me for every possible shift since.

Since *resigning*, any *anxiety* that I had felt before a shift, has now dissipated and *any snippy comments*, or people **power-tripping**, no longer really gets to me as much. I did, however, make the **mistake** of **befriending** someone who has worked there for **over 30 years** and is *extremely bitter and a little racist* (he had to do *sensitivity training* and all), who also happens to be a horse trainer. Whenever he is showing me how to do anything he says *"this is how I train my horses"* .... believe it or not, *Dear Journal*, but **I am not a horse.** He also gets super angry whenever management asks him to do anything. I think he was under the impression that I was leaving this job because I was **disgruntled**, but I did not actually have any real issue with anyone, simply a scheduling conflict.

Today was not the best day, I **fell twice** while running upstairs (what is wrong with me??) and had a very difficult person buying products in bulk, who was **outraged** that we had run **out of boxes**, proclaiming that I *"should not be giving away boxes like that"* and that it was ridiculous that I had to use bags instead, he could have come earlier.

That aside, with any self doubt and worry basically gone, I seem to have **found my footing** at this job and am starting to find the fun and camaraderie that I was craving. It also turns out that I am **awesome at up-selling** (*who knew?*) and *Management* has taken notice and have told me that they would like me to stay. I have figured out **a very particular route** around the store and have learned to bring a sweater with me so that nobody bothers me when I am on break (the questions are endless). Let me ask you, *Dear Journal*, if I can work out any scheduling conflicts, **do I give this more of a fair shot?** Also, **how do I ditch the bitter**

and racist guy? I am not sure if that is the best look for me!

Does this saga continue? Stay tuned...

The Retail Saga Part 2

Since my last entry, I did get more comfortable with the role. I started getting along with my coworkers a little bit better but in the back of my mind, I knew that **if I survived probation** and became permanent, **I would want to transfer to a smaller store**. In theory, a smaller store would entail **less work**, **less hours** and a **shorter commute**. I tried asking some of the long-term staff how I would request to transfer stores, but they *unsurprisingly* said that a smaller store would be a mistake and that I would have to stay where I was for six months anyway, and so I decided to leave it be.

Meanwhile, I had some more strange experiences (on top of the horse trainer). Between **a manager who started projectile vomiting right beside me**, while cashing me out (I have had my share of nights like those but was told it was likely food poisoning). A customer going crazy and **started breaking all the high-end products**, while running through the store, when security asked him to leave. I also made the mistake of asking a coworker how she hurt her back, after she called me over to lift heavy boxes for a customer. She told both me and the customer that if she lifted them herself it would be "*directly against doctors orders.*" Being naturally curious, I asked how she hurt her back, **she got so aggressive, repeatedly asking me "*why would you ask me that,*"** making me think that she was going to jump me, for having the audacity of asking. To this day, I do not know what happened to her back. Finally, I received **poor advice** and started letting calls from the store go to voicemail because I was told that if I turned the shift down, I would be **blacklisted**. It turned out that the person giving me the advice was **below me on the *seniority list* and was therefore taking all my shifts.**

On top of this, I won a contest and earned **two $200 gift cards** for raising so many charitable donations on behalf of the store. When I attempted to claim my prize, I was told that I must have *misunderstood the straightforward rules* and that the **person who hurt her back,** was going to calculate the top three fundraising people. I **really doubt** that I will be one of them after our intense encounter.

Despite all of this, I **survived my probation** and have officially become permanent staff, fancy name tag and all. I have yet to decide if this is a celebratory thing, as it is not the best job nor is it well paid, but an achievement, nonetheless.

I decided to take a risk and ask my manager **whether I could transfer stores**. It turned out to be a whole complicated procedure, where my request would have to be brought to various management levels. Also, I was then told that the manager at the store that I wanted to switch to, had a *"fiery explosive temper,"* so I decided I would not push it.

Meanwhile, I started to get back on the actual schedule and was having weekly shifts again. I got to make some cool displays, got competitive with charity donations once more, and was glad to see that some of my friends were also now permanent staff.

I had one shift where the local *Transit* was not running because of a **fire in the tunnel**, and I had to **walk the 20KM home**, in the sun while wearing boots, which reminded me why I wanted the transfer in the first place.

Coincidentally, the next week I got approval for the store transfer, and at the location that I wanted at that. It is funny how I went **from my resignation being demanded** to getting **transferred to the store I requested**. I was scheduled to start there two weeks later. I said all my dramatic goodbyes the first weekend and was *predictably* told repeatedly "*congrats, but this is a mistake, you do not want a smaller store...*" and to then later discover that I will indeed see them all once more at a shift the following week. Though, sadly, *due to management error*, **I was paid for neither of my final weeks.**

The new store location **has been great**, much less dramatic to get to and less political (thus far, anyway). It has been a busier store for me (which makes the shifts go faster), and lots of weird encounters. Including, one guy who it looked like was about **to throw sharp, *stabby* looking ice at me**, when he thought our "*negotiations were not going well*" after I told him that he could not return an item without a receipt (we were not negotiating). Another, who insisted on **trying to scan an item he bought elsewhere** because he wanted to "**see how it scans**," despite the lengthy line up behind him. Finally, the one who **pretended to throw an unopened can at me**, only for him to catch him last minute, as I ducked behind my cash register. **Is this retail experience really worth it?**

Does the saga continue? Stay tuned...

The Retail Saga Part 3

Life has been wild in the few months since my transfer. I am now working a crazy **20-25 hours a week** at this store (making my **total work week 50-55 hours**), unsurprisingly, I am now constantly exhausted. There is also a lot more *unhoused* individuals who come into this location, including one who comes into the store multiple times a day that I am convinced has *Scabies* or something similar and just as awful (you better believe that I am now constantly disinfecting my work area and sanitizing my hands). It is also a **high theft store**, where people will go as far as to fake stomach-aches just to squat down and hide something past security or buy something cheap after sneaking something more expensive into their bags (sadly, we do not always have the **A-Team Security** and I am sure not going to chase anyone).

I have also been having issues with my *Manager*, where he watches the clock whenever I arrive. He went so far as **offering** to provide me **mental health services** one day, after I was **two minutes late** (no need, I just missed a traffic light). He has also offered to train me on how to ask customers to take a survey when my survey numbers were not great (sure, show me how it is done).

All that aside though, these past few days have been wild and now we are back to debating on whether I quit. A few nights ago, it was the most customers that I have ever had, **293 people in four**

hours (that is roughly 74 people an hour and 1.5 people a minute), making me feel like I was the only one working there. The next night, we had **no security for over 3 hours** as both *Guards* watched someone they had **hogtied** to a chair for theft as they waited for the *Police* to arrive. Making me wonder why **two Security Guards** had to watch him, as people were literally walking out of the store with **bags full** of **unpaid items**. Just one day after that, I had to call *Security* myself for the first time as someone went around the store harassing everyone for money, including myself (no sir, that's called a robbery) with no *Guard* in sight.

Lately, I have been getting sick a lot more often (likely due to the above-mentioned *Scabies* and whatever other horrible diseases people are bringing into the store). Just over a month ago I was on antibiotics for **strep and a stomach infection** and then just two weeks ago I was fighting a **head cold** for over a week, for which I called in sick **two days in a row**. Old *Pippa* is just not built to deal with the public.

Then that brings us to the events of yesterday. I was not feeling overly well when I woke up and vomited before work (before you go thinking it, it would be a **real divine miracle** if it was *morning sickness*) but I thought it would pass. I also felt that I could not call in sick as I had just done that twice two weeks prior. I was **a minute early** for work (I see you checking your watch) and counted my *till* (which was 5 cents short). Everything was pretty normal except I still **felt really unwell**. I had to ask my *Backup* to cover me on cash on **three occasions**, as I went to go vomit (I was the only one who was supposed to stay on cash once again). **The forth time** that I started feeling nauseous, I thought that maybe I could wait until my break, which was scheduled to be in 40 minutes, and then just lie on the floor beside the toilet **for all 15 minutes** (the classy broad that I am). I had a customer and while exchanging pleasantries, I thought to myself that I **was not** going to make it to my break and that after this customer, I was going to need to go excuse myself once again. The customer was perfectly kind, and everything went normally and after she seemed to have left, I decided that I was **not** going to make it **all the way to the bathroom**, and I did not want to **stand in the middle of the store puking** and so I vomited into my garbage, which by the way **is a cardboard box**.

I then called for *Backup* and while I was doing that, I heard a sweet little *"have a nice day"* coming from behind me (ugh, **cringe**, I thought she left). My *Backup* arrived and caught the end of my **5th round** of sickness for that morning, she said that I looked really pale, while in the same breath telling me to get a garbage bag to clean it all up. When I came back with my garbage bag, my *Backup* had told my *Manager*, who asked me if I wanted to stay or go and I said that I was initially thinking that I would see how I felt after my break, but that I did not seem to be getting any better. I was then told to just go home, while I was crawling around on my hands and knees, cleaning my floor with disinfectant wipes. At least my *till* balanced though (except for the 5 cents missing from earlier).

Sadly, nobody has emailed me since yesterday morning to find out if I made it home okay. I could be hospitalized or dead for all they know (I realize that this is dramatic, but they did not even call me a taxi to ensure my safe arrival). Though, I suppose my *Manager* would have noticed that something was wrong, should I dare be **even a minute** late again.

Now, *Dear Journal*, is this job really worth it? Can I ever go back after today's embarrassment? Does this *Saga* continue? *Stay tuned...*

Part 6
Life Lessons and Inspirations in The City

The Journey to Driving

The driving licensing process where I am from is as follows. The **first step** ("*License 1*") is the written test. Once you pass that, you can **only drive** when accompanied by a fully licensed adult and **cannot drive** above 80KM per hour (no highway). The **next step** ("*License 2*") is the driving test, once you pass this, it is nearly the same as driving with a full license, except you cannot consume any alcohol. The **final step** is the full license, to get this you need to pass the *Highway Test*. The full process is supposed to take a maximum of **five years**.

My journey began like most driving journeys do, back in high school. The difference between myself and other keen teenagers, however, was that I had never really felt the pressure to get my driver's license. My high school was easily accessible by public transportation, and I think that the idea of driving simply made me nervous. Nevertheless, I took the written test for the sake of having some form of acceptable photo ID, besides my passport, and passed the first test quite easily.

I first felt the pressure to get my *License 2* when my younger family members started to take driving lessons. One in particular, *who is very close to my age*, seemed to fly through the driving test system with ease and so I felt inspired to sign up for lessons too. The in-class lessons were kind of fun and I made friends. The lesson package had included ten in-car lessons too. The first *Instructor* that I had, did not speak *English* particularly well and never made me feel comfortable enough **to go above 10 KM per hour** when driving (nor did he ever ask me to increase the speed, **even on busy roads**). I decided after eight lessons (I was not a confrontational person back then) that it was a waste of money and asked to change instructors. The next *Instructor* that I had, had also taught my family member and I had heard raving reviews about him. Although his communication skills were slightly better than the last *Instructor*, he would often grab my leg when he wanted me to slow down (I suppose that it is positive that I was now increasing my speed, but it is noteworthy that he **never used this** teaching method with my **male** family member). Regardless, he ended up making me feel like I was not a good driver, because I did not want to honk at a bicyclist that I was stuck driving behind (I did not want to startle said bicyclist).

By this point, I was now starting a summer job in *Small Town, Canada* and decided that my commute would be cut down by about 75% if I could just get my driver's license. Neither *Instructor* would let me use their car for the test (even though I am sure it was included in the initial lesson package, but that aside) so I used my family's car. I attempted this test a few times, the most memorable would include my first attempt, which became a clear fail, *to me anyway*, when the *Examiner* **pulled the handbrake up**, causing the car to **squeal**, when I was about to make a *right-hand turn* (which she deemed dangerous for

141

reasons still unknown). The next test of note was a **disaster** when I made a lane change straight through a **red light** (I hate lane changes). I decided that it was clearly just **not meant to be** and that it would be better to just commute the **three hours** to *Small Town*.

Roughly two years later, I realized that my license was **now expiring** [*please don't calculate my age*]. By this point, I had now lost a bunch of weight and I started to make a bit more effort on my appearance. It was becoming a problem to use my driver's license as my ID, as the photo no longer looked like me. When trying to get into *Night Clubs*, I would often be tested on my signature (which is different every time I write it) and *Postal Code* (which I had made up because I had just moved and did not know it at the time of writing the **License 1 test**) and decided that I would just rewrite the **test** and take a nicer photo (and correct my *Postal Code*). I do realize that I probably could have changed these things without rewriting the test, but the excuse made me feel better about the impending expiration, nonetheless. When writing the test, a man with *no hands* was also writing it beside me, and I spent a considerable amount of time wondering how he would hold the *steering wheel*, should he decide to drive (if he can do it, I can do it, right?), but I once again passed the **License 1 test**, despite this distraction.

I had now moved to the *City*, where everything was within walking distance and felt no real pressure to drive. Time moved on and eventually *my license was expiring again* [*please stop calculating*]. I always *felt a little embarrassed* about not having a driver's license, especially since there was now a **whole lineup** of *younger* relatives and friends with their driver's license, buying their own car. So I decided that I would try again. I took a bunch of lessons with a guy that I had found online, and he did pretty well with *building my confidence*, except that he had no time to teach me how to *parallel park* during my lessons. In fact, on test day, roughly **10 minutes before** my scheduled test time, he took a **toy car** out of his *glove compartment* to show me how to *parallel park,* his hand (obviously) being the road. During my test, I could not remember the *parallel parking* steps (or whatever he had shown me on his toy car) for the life of me and I *inevitably* **failed again**.

My friend had recently received her full license and highly recommended her *Instructor* and gave me his number. He was actually the **best *Instructor*** that I had ever had at this point, and it was the first time that I felt confident enough to actually take and pass the ***License 2 test***. The test was scheduled for the **day before my license was to expire again** [*I said don't calculate my age*]. On test day, I waited in the car for **over an hour** before the *Instructor* went inside the building to see what was wrong (I had to wait in the car), it turned out that the test centre had placed my paperwork in the wrong pile and finally someone came out to test me! **I PASSED**!! (Nailed that *parallel parking*

143

too) The **best part** was, it bought me **five more years** because my license was so close expiring (less than 24 hours). However, the *Instructor* tried to charge me **for an extra hour** because I had to wait so long for my test, since he had to cancel a lesson as a result (luckily, I did not have the extra cash on me). He said that I could pay him back when we practiced for my full license, but that day never came.

During those **five years**, I eagerly did some driving initially, and then some global travelling, and then *COVID* hit. Nobody was giving lessons during the height of lock-down and before I knew it, I got to the point where my license was about to expire again [*I said to stop calculating*]. I decided I did not want to start the process again, especially since I had a **really nice license photo**, which in fact looks better than I do now (after roughly 18 months of lock-down and quarantine and all). After scouring the internet and sifting through "virtual lessons" (which I did not think would cut it, unless the test was virtual (which would have been my preference, to be honest)) I finally found someone to give me in-car driving lessons. He was expensive and **only offered two-hour lessons**, which always felt too long but he did wonders to build my confidence, I even drove on the highway, which had become a bit of a **phobia** by this point.

When it was time to attempt my test, the *Examiner* that I had was cold right off the bat. He generally ignored me, had me pull over so that he could yell at someone for practicing parking in the *Test Centre* and **jumped up and cursed** when I accidentally **hit a curb** (the first time that I had ever done that and it was after being stopped at a stop sign, so I was not going very fast). I was always told that hitting the curb was an **automatic fail**, so I was not sure why we were even bothering with the highway portion of the test. At the end, the *Examiner* told me that what he failed me on was dangerous lane changes on the highway. I was now **three weeks away** from my license expiring and with the *COVID backlog*, I figured I would have to start again and had made peace with that.

By some miracle, I managed to secure a test date for the **day before my licence was expiring once again** (I seem to like that added pressure). I practiced and practiced and practiced, especially on those dreaded lane changes. I was so sick of my *Instructor* by this point, he was often late or spontaneously canceling on me, he would always end my lesson 15 minutes early, he would drop me off way out of the way after the lessons, and he was always lecturing me for **not** working **14 hour days** like he does, (I just do not want to work that much). I knew that I would be okay with not passing, especially since I knew that I could likely get the **License 2 easily** by this point (that nice ID photo though). I was planning to buy and practice in my own car if need be.

On test day **full licence - round 2**, my *Instructor* had me meet him at an out-of-the-way subway station at **6AM** (the test was scheduled for 8:20AM) and he showed up **15 minutes late**. We then had to drive roughly half an hour out of the way, *to pick up his other student* (why couldn't I get picked up from home too, though?) before heading to the *Test Centre*. The other student practiced his *License 2* route first (despite his later test time), and made it look so easy (why did I struggle so much?). He did steer by aggressively turning the wheel with the palm of his hand though, and I was always told that was a *no-no*. When it was then my turn to practice, there was only time for me to practice the route once, after all of that messing around, but I knew that after all of that stress, **I had to pass**. The *Examiner* came quickly, and I did my test. At the end of the test the *Examiner* said to park anywhere, and the spot that I had chosen had a guy pacing back and forth while on the phone in front of it. This caused the *Examiner* to **frustratingly** remind me that she had said to park **anywhere** (all of that and I fail on my bad parking spot choice) and so I chose a different spot. She said that I did a really good job on the test and that, most importantly, **I PASSED!!!!!!!**

My *Instructor* then came running over to tell me that I passed because I got the **"*easy Examiner*"** and I do not know if that's true, **or if it was from**:

- The insane amount of practice that I did;
- If it's because I walked barefoot in a field the day before to manifest a pass; or
- If I simply drove well.

What I do know is:

- I probably spent **more money** on lessons than anyone else in the country;
- I got to keep my nice driver's license photo;
- I owe **a huge thank you** to my friends and family for their patience and for teaching me what they know, and answering my constant questions; and
- Until I am **80** years old, and the ***Government*** is inevitably trying to pry my driver's license out of my cold, insane, dying hands, I **never** have to go through this again [*and yes, that is still a number of years away, thank you*]. Nor do I ever have to drive again, if I choose not to.

Persistence pays off.

Stitches

One morning, I decided to go for a run. It was a particularly nice *August* morning, and I did the thing that I never do (as a non-morning person) and got out of bed to finish my run **before work** (I was rather proud of myself). I was only trying to do "*3n1s*" that morning, if you are unsure about this training method, it is apparently the best way to learn to run. That day I was doing three minutes of running and one minute of walking and then I increase the length of my run every week (I started out with "*1n1s*"). I found this to be a helpful method back when I was *marathon training* (*humble flex*) (but we will cover this another time).

That morning I found the run particularly **torturous and challenging** (I actually **hate running**, never experienced that *runner's high* people talk about, I just liked challenging myself and the training community). There was a small **staircase** on my route, that I knew was there, but it really blended in well with the sidewalk. As I was approaching it, I managed to misjudge how close it in fact was and **went flying off the three steps** and slid along the pavement. I laid there for a minute and thought to myself "*why does my life have to suck*". I suddenly noticed a lady approaching me from the distance, I **leapt up** and pretended that I was fine. Interestingly, since this, they have added railings and painted a yellow stripe on each step, it could not have been just me (I really wish I had sued *the City*).

148

I embarked on the short walk home. As I was walking, I started feeling *lightheaded* and like I was going to faint. I sat down on the sidewalk curb for a minute to examine what I thought were my only injuries, the cuts on my knees. I could not believe that I had injured them again (I felt like I had just got them back into working order). I unfortunately did not bring my phone with me, but I could see construction workers nearby and I was tempted to ask them if I could use a towel or something (or sit and look cute in hopes that they will offer to help me) but I decided just to brave the five-minute walk.

When I finally made it home and looked in the mirror, I saw my elbow for the first time and realised that there was a huge gash and that I was leaving **a trail of blood** around my tiny (***jail cell sized***) apartment. I decided that it was likely fine and just needed a shower and a band-aid. I got halfway through my shower and started feeling really lightheaded once again. Not wanting to faint in the shower, I got out with ***shampoo still in my hair*** and sent my workplace a message to inform them that I had an accident, and I went back to bed.

I woke up feeling a little better and decided that I would go to my local walk-in clinic (my *eye candy doctor*) to see if I needed stitches or something, though I did feel like a **hypochondriac** for going. I attempted to finish my shower, when I realised that **my water had been turned off**. When I asked my *Landlord* what happened, as there was no prior warning (did I forget to pay a bill?), she said that it was because of some sort of pipe emergency (likely caused by those unhelpful workers). So I went to the *clinic* with my hair half washed and my arm still covered in mud.

As luck would have it, my *eye candy doctor* was not overly busy and could see me straight away. He asked me to do various arm tests so he could **see if it was broken**, this felt unnecessary to me, as I already felt like I was overreacting for being there (having not really seen my elbow myself). My *eye candy doctor* told me that I had to go to the *Hospital* and get stitches because it needed a deep clean and he did not have the necessary tools. He did not write me a note (which caused problems later) and so I went to the *Hospital*.

I went through the *Triage* and the nurse who saw me was also a runner and understood what I was talking about when I described what happened (or at least was kind enough to pretend to understand). I went through all the initial steps rather quickly and made it into my room to wait. There was a guy in the room across from me, **who arrived after me** and was seen straight away. Apparently, he slept with his contacts in his eyes and was concerned that he now had *an ulcer in his eye* (which sounds dreadful). **He did not.** Then *finally* it was my turn. The doctor gave me a hard time about not having a doctor's note (for reasons unknown), and at first was unsure whether I needed stitches at all (I am not leaving here empty-handed **after a three hour wait**, doctor) and basically informed (*lectured*) me that a good cleaning with soap and water can go a long way (thanks, but I had no running water). He then agreed that I did need stitches after-all and he would need to clean my elbow with equipment used in *the OR* (long swabs) and went off to get the equipment.

In his **lengthy absence**, there was an announcement for a "*Code Black*" on the intercom system. I thought that this meant that someone had overdosed, which would not have been overly surprising, given where the *Hospital* was located, however, after conducting a *Google* search, I have recently learned that a "*Code Black*" means **a bomb threat to the facility.** This begs the question of **why I was stuck waiting in the room while the doctor was running to safety.**

No bomb exploded (to my knowledge) and the doctor eventually *and no doubt reluctantly* returned. He froze my arm, and he did the deep clean (it took about 10 swabs to get all the debris out), which was very uncomfortable. I then got stitches down my elbow and had to have them removed the following week. I tried to go into work and brave it out in the afternoon, but my elbow got more and more painful as the freezing wore off, so I went home instead. When I later had the stitches removed with my *eye candy doctor*, he said that he would have done a much nicer job with the stitches, which would have **left a much smaller scar** (*why didn't you then?*).

It took a long time to recover from this accident. I got into *boxing* fitness classes for a while afterwards, and any planks or any pressure on my elbow **really burned**, so I had to wear elbow padding. I initially thought that maybe my elbow was *infected* and that is why it burned, but I was told that it was likely **just nerve damage**. It thankfully is pretty well all recovered, though my *eye candy doctor* was correct about **the nasty scar.**

As for lessons learned:

1.   Mornings are always terrible, just sleep in;

2.   Do not run on an empty stomach, especially if you are already feeling off;

3.   Try avoiding any accidents on days that your water is turned off;

4.   Ensure that you have that doctor's note; and

5.   If there is a *Code Black* in a *Hospital*, get out of there!

My Best Diets

With the holidays coming and the majority finding that they are putting on the "**Quarantine 15**", here are my **top three diets** that worked for me. I have lost 45-70 pounds **three times** in my life and although, I have put the weight back on twice, I did like how I looked in photos during the lower weight times.

The First, my easiest "*lifestyle change*" was when I was 21. I was at my heaviest (size 14) and decided that I wanted to lose weight. The original goal was to become a size 7, because I thought that this was the perfect size.

At the time, my diet consisted of at least one bagel and cream cheese a day and one or two iced cappuccinos (*I love them*). I could also probably finish a carton of Fruitopia and a row of cookies. It was all delicious, but I felt that I could likely do better.

I originally was going to try and be like a celebrity and stick to lemon water and raw veggies, but this lasted a week and was **not sustainable**. However, this *starvation week* made me feel so guilty if I ate junk food, that I just stopped.

My daily bagels became one "6-inch sub" a day (because I read somewhere that bagels were equivalent to five slices of bread, and I decided that I should not eat more than two slices of bread.

However, I am no longer **sure how true** this is…but believed it at the time.).

Iced Caps became Coke Zero.

Cookies became low calorie hot chocolate.

Basically, anything that I ate became the low-calorie version of same.

This worked for me. I lost **50 pounds** in 8 months. I surpassed my size 7 goal and became a **size 3**. I felt great about myself.

I even started walking everywhere. This was before I had a *"Fitbit"*, and those **10,000 steps were not mandatory.**

Throughout this first journey, I made friends with *"the Model"* and (*ironically*) – gained it all back…more will follow about this *"**lifestyle**"* in a future blog. All I can say is that it is way more fun to put on weight than it is to lose it.

The Second, my most restricting and most successful diet. ***The "Dukan Diet"***.

The Model and I were no longer friends and throughout this *"fun"* party journey, I gained roughly **40 pounds back** – still not at my largest but close. I thought that I could feel better about myself, the fallout and everything else, if I could just look amazing again.

The *Dukan Diet* worked well. However, I admittedly got a bit obsessive and had a hard time moving beyond "**Phase 2**" of the *diet* (that is, alternating between veggie days and protein days). I was afraid of moving to "**Phase 3**" (you can eat salad and protein every day except for one day a week where you just have a protein day) you move to this phase once you reach your "*goal weight*". Every time I reached my *goal weight*, I made a new goal – in order to have "*wiggle room*". I went down to a **Size Zero**. My coworkers all thought that I was sick and **lost too much weight**. They may have been right, but it felt great to hear, nonetheless.

Eventually, I signed up for a night school course in order to have an excuse to buy a **cheat meal** after work on school nights and chill with my restrictions just a little bit. '**Cheat night**' eventually became **cheat weekend,** which inevitably led to the *Dukan* life being over and the weight creeping back on.

The Third is my current journey. It was inspired when I joined a *boxing gym* and asked the *Coach* for tips on how to skip rope on one of my first days at the gym. The *Coach*, trying to be helpful, said that I looked to be about **200 pounds** and to **pretend** to be **120 pounds**. She said that this will help me feel lighter and therefore jump higher – in my head I was still **120 pounds**. This was a bit eye opening; I knew I had likely **gained a little bit** of weight (the size zero pants just did not fit as well...*but maybe they shrunk?*) but I did not realize that I looked like I was 200 pounds to those around me. For the record, not that it really matters to anyone but me, but I was **never 200 pounds**, although close.

This time, I did not want to do the *Dukan* because, although it was very successful for me, I wanted to have the energy to go to the gym and to go running two-three times a week, and despite how much weight I lost on the *Dukan*, I also found it draining.

I started running (trained for a 10km charity run) and I signed up with a *Personal Trainer*, in order to learn the basic gym fundamentals (use weights, squat and lunges, etc.) I **highly recommend** signing up with a *Personal Trainer*, especially if you are unsure of what to do at the gym or in a fitness class. It was great.

I cut down on carbs and anything with higher sugar and/or calories really. However, I am allowed these things now and then, I did not want to be too restricting because I am **tired** of that **"yo-yo life."**

This has been a very slow process, I think it's partly because I am **older** now and my **metabolism** is just not where it was. Sometimes the slow weight loss pace does bring me down. However, I have lost roughly **45 pounds** in the last year, including **10 pounds in quarantine** (*how many people can say that?*). I have gone down from about a size 10-12 to a **size 4**.

My BMI – which, to my surprise, had me in the **overweight** category before my current journey, is now in the **middle of the normal category**.

The best part is, I feel a lot more **confident** in myself than I did before this journey.

So what have I learned thus far?

- Putting the weight back on is a lot more fun than taking it off.
- It is so important to learn the fundamentals in weight training to get the full benefits of a fitness class.
- Super effective diets does not always mean better.
- Abs are difficult to get – even with a Personal Trainer...
- and, as the old Kate Moss saying goes, *"nothing tastes as good as skinny feels."*

...oh and, after a lot of practice, I did also eventually learn how to skip rope.

My Best Diets Part 2

I wrote my last diet post in *October 2020*. At that time, I had very proudly lost **10 pounds** in spite of *lockdown*. I was doing at home workouts, running twice a week and I was pretty much eating *carb free*, as much as possible. What feels like immediately after writing it, I had to take a break from working out and running. I had horrendous **shin splints** that were becoming **stress fractures** and was also diagnosed with **arthritic toes**, after I went to see about a shooting pain. This is on top of **never ending shoulder pain**, that I have been complaining about for as long as I can remember.

But no worries...I started *Physiotherapy* and *Acupuncture*. The *Acupuncture* had amazing results for my toes, the shin splints were a longer recovery process. However, there was no change in my shoulders.

I was on the mend, I was doing fewer intensive workouts and had given up on including weights while working out but at least my diet was still intact. My weight had plateaued after that 10 pound loss, which was a little unmotivating, but that is better than gaining weight, **right?**

Then came the *Strep Throat*. It was horrible, I have had it at least a dozen times in my life and was actually looking into getting my tonsils removed *Pre-Covid* but apparently that is quite a difficult feat for adults. I decided to take a break from the diet and just ate whatever I wanted because I was already feeling crappy, so why not? I do realize that this was a little ironic considering the very sore throat, you would think that I would just stick with soup. I also could not go out and socialize or grocery shop really, as a sore throat and fever are *Covid* symptoms, so I had to order more takeout anyway. In fact, when I picked up my *antibiotics*, the *Pharmacist* used a literal basket on a stick to pass it to me and strongly recommended getting a *Covid test*, but this was before they were so easily accessible.

Okay, that is fine. Eating more takeout, on a break from the diet, feeling crappy, it was winter by this point, and I did not want to go outside anyway. I should just lie in bed and eat comfort food for now. Except *"for now"* never ended. I probably **gained the 10 pounds** back by *December 2020*, but *you know* at least ***it shook the plateau*** and it will be easier to get back on track with faster results (by losing that extra 10 pounds). In theory, it will make me more motivated.

2021 rolled around. The start of a new and better year, there were a lot of beautiful births in 2021, which was lovely to see. By this point, I still had not gone back to my *Physiotherapy* since my *Strep Throat* episode because I simply got lazy. I was also feeling unmoved about getting back into working out, as *lockdowns* were continuously being lifted and then placed back again, **like some sort of endless tease.**

Not only that, but on a separate note, my annual work review did not play out the way that I had hoped. As a result of a staff shortage, I was **assisting nine people for three months** at my crappy office job, *which went unnoticed*, so I was starting to think about leaving for other opportunities. I also had one intense boss, who expected me to go into the office **during the height of** *lockdown* to do her 10 year-old filing, that she kept bringing into the office and dumping on my desk, in order to clean her house. This was back when offices were being spontaneously inspected to ensure that **only essential workers** were there, and everything was already scanned and saved in the system anyway. Personally, I would not have considered filing stale documents to be essential. *But ok let's risk my life, that's fine*. I did end up signing up for an evening virtual boxing class in hopes that it would jumpstart my fitness. Even though the class was fun, the shoulder pain and general exhaustion made it very difficult to inspire myself to log in.

I then had a spontaneous allergy attack and broke into full hives for reasons unknown, but it made breathing difficult, and I was always congested. Whatever allergy medication that I was on, caused me to get severely bloated fast.

I also tragically and unexpectedly lost a beloved family member. Which has been very difficult to bounce back from.

Despite all of this, I was still expected to go into the office to file old documents during yet another full lockdown and my bereavement period.

Needing a change of scene, I got myself a fancy new job later in the year and they had enforced the mandatory vaccine policy shortly after I started my employment. I had three weeks to get double dosed or get fired. I reacted horribly both times (as I knew I would) and ended up needing an *inhaler* (note: I am not blaming the vaccine, the cause is unclear). I could not breathe well and as a result started walking less. The new job was very demanding, and I was eating more, **it is not even that I was eating more**, I was eating more takeout and higher calorie but delicious comfort meals. I was also snacking much more than I used to (*but chips and dip is delicious*). There was **zero work/life balance** in this new role, and I had no time to myself to workout, even if I had wanted to. **I hated the job and the constant pressure that I was under, but at least the pay was better.**

I then got fired. It was shocking but not surprising (if that makes sense to anyone besides me). It took a hit on my self-esteem and any remaining confidence that I had (I do have an excellent support system though). I was highly stressed and hyper focused on finding a new job, which ended up taking a long three months. However, the new position is much less demanding and there is no physical filing (thank goodness).

This spring 2022, with wedding season approaching, being tired of being exhausted and out of breath all the time and the annoyance of none of my clothes fitting, I decided it was time to get back on track. I did the very hard thing and stepped on the scales, to see where I was at, and the number **was humbling.** I checked my *BMI*, mostly out of curiosity, and that was **even more humbling**.

My first goal was that I wanted to rewire how I think about what to eat but to also not be *too restrictive*. I decided I would try the *One Meal a Day Diet*, it is similar to *Intermittent Fasting* but I have small and healthy snacks throughout the day because I knew that it was not realistic for me to go all day without eating. I also did not want my one meal be **10,000 calories**, so I try and be more calorie conscious in my food decisions. I decided to also try out the *Glucose Goddess* theory. The *Goddess* recommends starting every meal with veggies, eat your protein second and then eating carbs last. This way you are coating your intestines and there is less of an insulin spike, causing less sugar cravings. It is highly controversial as it encourages *ritual eating*, and I have no idea if it actually works, but I figured that starting my meal with veggies is not the worst thing I could do.

I also started going to the gym again, roughly 3-4 times a week. I aim for times that I think I will be alone because I was afraid of being judged, but there are roughly five regular and encouraging people that I am starting to recognize. I increase the speed and resistance on the *Treadmill* every week, and I am now at about five kilometers in distance. I also increase the amount of time that I am on the *Stair Master,* during my first week at the gym, I really struggled with completing five minutes on the *Stair Master* and this week I am at 17 minutes.

I am not at my goal yet, but I am **down 4 sizes,** my BMI is in a healthier place, and according to my *Fitbit,* my heart is healthier too. I do still have **a very long road ahead** of me and I look forward to updating you, once I reach my goal. As a bonus, I find myself less congested too. I do find it frustrating that I let myself go so far down the *Rabbit Hole,* but at the same time, that same **heavier person** is also the one who decided to do something about it and push through during those really difficult first few weeks. ***How can I be mad at her?***

I suppose the point of this whole entry is, is that there is life after lockdown (let us all keep that in mind, when we are inevitably endlessly locked down once more for the next *Covid Winter Wave*) and **it is never too late to begin again.**

Left-Handed Inspiration

When I was in *College*, there was a lady named *Berta*, who happened to be in all of my classes and (*annoyingly*) happened to get employed before me when we graduated (*not relevant, though*).

Berta was an older lady, maybe in her 60s, (one of the second career folks in my classes), who wore hot pink short-shorts daily and a green vest, *a fisherman looking vest* with several pockets, every day. Each of those pockets seemed to contain enough change for her extra-large coffees. *Berta* would always come into a class with one coffee per hour of that class [e.g. a three-hour class would require a tray of three coffees]. *Berta* was always early for class, often gossiping with the other early birds (*never with me, though*), usually about whatever date she had that weekend [*Berta* had a more active dating life than I did].

One morning, she was talking about being **left-handed,** (being a fellow *lefty*, my ears naturally perked up), and about how left-handed people generally die first (I did not know this), as the world was built for right-handed people. Anyways, I found it quite inspiring, here's for some **inspiration**:

Apparently, when *Berta* was five years old, she was climbing a tree and when she got to the top, she fell to the ground. The tree was **nine feet tall,** and *Berta* walked away **without a scratch**. She read in the paper a few days later, that a kid had fallen from that same tree and died.

Berta then caught Scarlett Fever when she was seven years old. The Family Doctor paid a house visit and told Berta's parents that they can either give Berta a bath, or put her straight to bed, but the Doctor advised that either way **Berta would be dead in the morning**. Berta clearly survived the night and as she said, "I'm still standing, where is the Doctor now?" (I mean, probably dead of old age but anyway).

In her 20s, Berta was apparently riding her bicycle, and somebody suddenly opened their car door in her bike path, and she went flying off of her bicycle and broke her arm. It could have been much worse. Berta reckons that she should have died, especially considering that she had to hitchhike with a truck driver in order to get to the hospital.

So, as her conclusion, Berta proclaimed *"the world might be built for right-handed people, but lefties know how to get back up when they fall!"*

I was cheering by the end!

Manufactured by Amazon.ca
Bolton, ON

40315737R00097